Why I Killed
Gandhi?

Why I Killed Gandhi?

NATHURAM GODSE

·nAMASKAR
BOOKS
happy reading to you

Published by
NAMASKAR BOOKS
Building No. 2/42 (Second Floor)
Ansari Road, Daryaganj
New Delhi-110002
e-mail: namaskarbooks@gmail.com
Website: www.namaskarbooks.com

ISBN: 978-93-5571-592-0

Why I Killed Gandhi?
By Nathuram Godse

Edition 2023

Price
₹ 200.00 (Rupees Two Hundred only)

Printed at Japan Art, Delhi

Contents

Preface

Mohandas Karamchand Gandhi, appeared on the scene of Indian politics in approximately 1915 and dominated it until the afternoon of January 30, 1948 when the three bullets fired by Nathuram Vinayak Godse ended his life. Nathuram Godse surrendered to the authorities.

At the famous Red Fort trial in Delhi on November 8, 1948, the special judge of the court asked Nathuram what he had to say regarding the case against him. Not as a defendant. 1, Nathuram Godse produced a detailed statement in response. It is this statement in court that is presented here.

There was a ban on the publication of his statement, and it had a peculiar antecedent. Shri CKDaphtary, the chief prosecutor, asked the court not to allow the defendant Nathuram Godse read the statement he had prepared and submit only the explanation of the charges against him. This request had a purpose. The Prosecutors discovered that by confessing to the murder charges, Nathuram I would like to bring to light and witness all the commissions and omissions, promises and deceptions, not only from Gandhi but also from the party in power, which he was going to present as the reason behind his act and thus make the truth public through the court process, which the prosecution wanted to stop from the beginning. Judge Shri Atma Charan asked Shri Daphtary:

How can I stop the accused from testifying? According to the defendant there might be in his defense some justification for his act. Or, it could there are reasons to reject the charges. Show me if you have any authority or case law that supports your objection.

Shri Daphtary had to admit that he had no such jurisprudence or authority that could quote. The court denied the objection and allowed Nathuram Godse to proceed with the reading your statement.

The next day, the press had excerpts from the statement. Both class intelligent as the masses that had been kept in darkness came to know the Nathuram Godse's posture. They also learned that he had not denied the charge of assassinate Gandhiji.

Pandit Nehru was the Prime Minister. Under his direction, state by state banned the publication of the declaration, in part or in full.

It can be noted that the government became wiser when Nathuram Godse completed his arguments before the High Court in Simla in June 1949. So soon as the judges returned to their chambers, the police pounced on the reporters, he snatched his notebooks and tore them to pieces. They threatened those who engaged in true report.

There is a persistent lawsuit over Nathuram Godse's statement in court.

This was published in English, the language in which it was made before the court.

People around the world have been curious to know about connected people with the episode of Gandhi's death. They wonder what kind of men they were and from what ilk Some "reputable" writers have ventured into the subject. In doing so, they have distorted data, lies replaced by facts, have indulged in innuendo malicious in essence, and created filthy innuendo in his so-called literary works. Have resorted to cheap sensationalism to please the mood of readers and distort history.

That aside, the authentic statement will clear up the atmosphere of doubt and find dishonest versions of some writers made to tarnish your image. The readers they could form their own assessment of the sheer facts and the mere statement. I quote Nathuram himself, Honest historians will put my act up for consideration and they will find the true value of it some day in the future.

The law gives a special kind of sanctity to "dying statements." Nathuram Godse, in the circumstances in which it was performed, commends no less than a holiness.

The author (Gopal Godse) is the younger brother of Nathuram Godse, and was also accused in the Gandhi murder case. He was found guilty of conspiracy and sentenced to exile for life. He was released from prison in October 1964, but was arrested for new account a month later under the Indian Defense Act and remained in prison for more than a year. He was finally released in late 1965.

This book seeks to present the statement of Nathuram Vinayak Godse at the trial of Red Fort in its entirety. Before that, an introduction to the events, details of investigations and the formation of the special court. The procedure is presented after the declaration was completed, the trial, appeals and events up to the November 15, 1949 when Nathuram and Apte were executed. After that, shows a profile of Nathuram Vinayak Godse and the other defendants, as well as the thoughts of the author while serving sentence. As an epilogue, some words on whether future events only confirmed or found some discrepancy in the statement along with the effect of the application of Gandhian policies on the nation. A translation of Nathuram's testament appears at the end.

By his own will, Nathuram Godse bequeathed to Dattatraya, the younger brother, the right to publish the statement, who in turn kindly assigned the right to the author, for which he is grateful.

The author gratefully acknowledges the help given by the editors to bring out this book.

September 19, 1993   (Gopal Godse)

The Events

With separation from India granted, on August 15, 1947, British rule reached its end, and the two dominions, India (truncated) and Pakistan took shape. There was a large scale of population migration with incalculable violence, death, looting, rape among others stuff. The suffering of the refugees, and of the Hindus in particular presented a pitiful sight, and here every action of Gandhiji was pro-Muslim and anti-Hindu. The integration of the states would take place. With Nizam of Haiderabad, things were far to be quiet and Kashmir was under attack.

Sardar Vallabhbhai Patel was then the Vice Prime Minister of India. The pay of cash balances of fifty-five tens of million rupees that were owed to Pakistan at the time of separation from India was one of the main issues to discussion and negotiation with Pakistan. Inevitably, the matter was linked to the Pakistani aggression in Kashmir. In the statement made by Sardar Patel before the press conference on January 12, 1948, presented the case of India in terms unequivocal. He said:

We were fully justified in taking precautions against actions aggressive towards Kashmir by postponing the implementation of the agreement. He The agreement does not require the government of India any fixed date for payment. Of Pakistan is in no way justified in insisting on our payment of balances of cash. I made it very clear that we would not agree to any payment until the Kashmir matter was resolved.

Consequently, Sardar Vallabhbhai Patel was sought to withhold the payment of fifty-five tens of million rupees to Pakistan until the Kashmir affair was resolved.

There are two ways to put out a fire: One is to throw water on it and the other is to cut the supply of substances that feed it. Our army was doing its best effort to stop the invaders in Kashmir and drive them out. This war of strategy in financial transactions by the government of India (retaining the payment) was valuable, because it was necessary to keep the material that it could possibly serve as fuel. In these circumstances, the decision of thegovernment of India at the time to withhold the payment of 55 million rupees until the Kashmir affair being resolved was commendable. It was a wise solution to stop the Kill immediately and establish peace. Two decades later, the march of the Indian army to Lahore to defend against the invasion of Pakistan in Kashmir under the leadership of the Prime Minister Shastriji was as timely as he was commendable.

In those hectic days, Gandiji was in the city of Delhi. Who occupied the high ranks of the government of India used to meet with him and discuss business politicians. Gandhiji did not approve of this government decision. Gandhiji believed that by blocking Pakistan in this way were diverting their way to Ahimsa. January 12 1948, Gandhiji threatened the government saying that until they annul the decision before mentioned and paid the money to Pakistan, would go on a hunger strike. It can get a suggestion from a portion of the sermon given by Gandhiji on January 12, 1948, where he tried to persuade the government of India to reverse his decision, but failed. He had said:

But the time comes when a worshiper of Ahimsa is forced to begin fasting to express to society its opposition to any injustice. The does because being a worshiper of Ahimsa has no other way open for him. Such a critical moment has come for me.

Sardar Patel's steadfastness must have forced Gandhiji to pronounce such words of despair. On the other hand, Sardar Patel did not like the Gandhiji's resolution to go on a hunger strike. This is what Maulana Azad has said in your book. Sardar Patel left Delhi. On January 13, 1948, Gandhiji began his fast.

The net result of Gandhiji's fast was that around January 17, the government gave up and agreed to pay the money to Pakistan, ending the policy from Sardar to Kashmir.

The government of India issued a press release (on or around January 17 1948) which reads as follows:

In view of the request made by Gandhiji to the nation, the government has decided to remove the only cause of suspicion and friction between the two States, which consequently with national honor and national interest, are in his power to remove.

They do this spontaneous show in the hope that it will help produce an atmosphere of goodwill for which Gandhiji is suffering a crucifixion of the body and thus guide this great servant of the nation to end their fast and add even more to their unmatched services towards India.

The government has decided to immediately implement the financial agreement with Pakistan regarding cash balances.

Despite all this overflowing generosity and goodwill on the part of the government Indian Pakistani heart did not soften. The Kashmir problem continued.

Nathuram Vinayak Godse and Narayan Dattatraya Apte ran a diary with the name "Hindu Rashtra", which was an old "Agrani" in a new suit. Since before 15 August 1947, as the predictive signs of the creation of a Muslim state founded on the communal principle on the very Indian soil were demonstrating every day that As it happened, the editors of this newspaper became more and more scathing and critical. There were even loss orders for the two security deposits of 3,000 rupees each.

On Seeing the news on the ticker on January 12, 1948, that Gandhiji would begin his fasting, it became clear to Nathuram Godse that this act was contemplated to press the government of India to reverse its decision to withhold payment of fifty-five tens of millions of rupees. By this time his bitter feelings towards Gandhiji and his continuing anti-Hindu role reached its climax. As soon as you read the news about Gandhiji's fast on the ticker, Nathuram must have thought that any other plan he had to step aside, he had to take charge to make sure that Gandhiji did not interfere with the democratic work of the government; for that reason, the task of assassinating Gandhiji it had to be done first and he had to risk it all, because according to Nathuram it was a life and death problem for the nation.

On January 20, 1948, a bomb exploded during the afternoon prayer of Gandhiji close to the ground for prayer. Madan Lal Pahwa was apprehended at the scene. He he was one of the victims of partition. The police obtained information that Madan Lal had other accomplices in the conspiracy, that the plan had not worked and that his conspirators had fled. As a consequence, the government strengthened the police force and security measures at Casa Birla. The police spread a network across India to arrest others. However, for the next ten days, the police were unable to do no progress in apprehending the others.

And then, on January 30, 1948, at five o'clock in the afternoon, when Gandhiji, accompanied by a paraphernalia, was about to reach the ground to pray located in the enclosure of House Birla, Nathuram Vinayak Godse fired three shots at point-blank range. Gandhiji, with a faint "ah," possibly a muscle reflex, fell to the ground. Stayed instantly unconscious and breathed his last breath twenty minutes later. After having fired, Nathuram raised his hand with the gun and called the police. Gave up voluntarily before the authorities.

From the beginning, Nathuram Godse was fully aware that after the assassination of Gandhiji at his hands political powers of the moment would assign him all kinds of attributes, such as fanatic, maniac, lunatic, and so many others.

That's why who formally wanted it to be officially registered by the authorities corresponding at the same time to verify that he did not suffer from any illness, neither mental nor physical, and that his mental state did not fit any definition of mental disorder, illness or aberration. The request made by Nathuram to the doctor that was brought in for examination shortly after his arrest following the murder of Gandhiji was:

Doctor, please examine me completely and register scrupulously if my pulse and my heart work normally. The doctor did so and declared that his heart and pulse were beating normally.

After his surrender and arrest, Nathuram remained in detention for some time in a cell on Tughlaq Road and was later transferred into custody to Parliament Street. Together with the authorities, some other people also went to see him. Nathuram walked from back and forth in the cell, but sometimes he was close to the bars. Noticing the gaze of an individual stopped near the bars and asked:

You are Shri Devadas Gandhi, I suppose.

Yes, but how did you recognize me?

Was that individual's question. Perhaps you expected to find a monster with hideous appearance and bloodlust, without a trace of education. The gentle and clear words of Nathuram and his composure were quite incongruous with what he expected to see.

We have recently met at a press conference. You were there as the editor of The Hindustan Times.

And you?

I am Nathuram Vinayak Godse, the editor of the Hindu Rashtra newspaper. Me I was also present there. Today you have lost your father and I am the cause of that tragedy. I am very sorry for the loss that has befallen you and the rest of your family. Really believe me. It did not motivate me to this no personal hatred, no resentment, no evil intention towards you.

Seeing that a man, whose bloodstained hands had not yet dried, was talking to him in a way as calm and balanced as a third party could speaking, Shri Devadas Gandhi's curiosity aroused. There would be nothing out of the ordinary if he felt intense contempt for his father's murderer. If I felt that, at least I didn't showed back then, and putting aside for a moment the personal grief for the death of his father, he asked Nathuram, "Then why did he do it?" Nathuram replied, "The reason is purely political and only political. Would you listen to me by half an hour or less? Kindly ask the officer for permission. As you are editor soon you will understand the background ". The police did not allow any more talk.

❑

The Police Investigation;
The Arrests and the Special Court

Nathuram Godse turned himself in to authorities at the scene. The investigation began that same night. People made wild guesses as long as the name of Nathuram. Te refugees were restless, fearing that Gandhiji's assassin it could be one of them. Nathuram's name was subsequently revealed and it became clear that he was neither a Punjabi, nor a Bengali, nor a Sindhi, and not even a refugee. Joy was openly expressed in cities like, Amritsar, Ambala, Calcutta, Kanpur, among others.

Digamber Ramchandra Badge was arrested by the Pune Police on 31 December 1948 and was later brought under the command of the Bombay Police.

Thousands of people across the country were arrested under Detention laws Preventive VD Savarkar was also one of them. Then, apparently for reasons cited in the chapter concerning Savarkar, Savarkar's arrest went from being a low the Act of Preventive Detention to one in which he was accused of the murder of Gandhi.

Ten days before the murder, Madan Lal Pahwa had already been arrested at the time of the January 20 bomb explosion. I had nothing to add to the information that had given in the investigation related to it.

Monday morning, that is, February 2, 1948, when I (Gopal Godse) I said goodbye to my wife and left the house, I gave her an idea of the possibility of being arrested any time. At that time, I had established my residence in Khadki, a suburb from Pune. On February 5, 1948, I left Khadki for Kamshet. I got off in Kamshet me I headed to Uksan which was ten miles from Kamshet. I still wasn't halfway there when I saw the police van following me. They took me in their vehicle.

On February 6, 1948 in Bombay, Badge's servant, Shankar Kistayya, entered to the Office of the Criminal Investigation Department. The last to be arrested were Nana Apte and Karkare, whom the police arrested in Bombay on 13 and 14 February 1948. Dr. Parchure de Gwalior was arrested and held prisoner in the Gwalior fort.

On May 25, 1948, all of us who were kept in the Office of the Criminal Investigation Department. Like Savarkar not felt fine, they brought him to Delhi the next day, that is, May 26, 1948 Arthur Highway Prison.

On May 27, 1948, we were ushered into the entrance of the special prison at Fort Red, and it was there that everyone, including Savarkar and Dr. Parchure, met.

Badge had become a snitch before the agreed date for the next audience. After that, he was never called to court again.

In 1947, the Bombay Legislature passed a law known as the Act of Bombay Public Safety Measures (Act IV of 1947) with provisions such such as the appointment of a Special Court, the appointment of a single judge with authority To examine the evidence, leaving aside the conventional procedure, the worksheets charge and charges, to issue a death sentence or perpetual exile, for attempted homicide, to carry out the processing without delay, as well as to reduce the period of appeal from 60 to 15 days. This process was related to the extent that the Act was applicable in the province of Delhi in 1948.

From the gloomy and stale atmosphere of solitude we arrived at the open environment of the Court. It was half past nine in the morning on May 27, 1948. The atmosphere in the Corte was even more invigorating. The courtroom was a hallway that measured about a hundred feet long and twenty-two wide, and was in the first floor.

The Gandhi murder case had become as important and serious as the incident itself. One of the reasons was that the Government involved in this conspiracy none other than the internationally known Swantantryaveer Savarkar, Savarkar, who for most of his life had organized secret societies for the liberation of the India of slavery inside and outside the country; he who endured incomparable suffering, harassment and torture in that attempt; and he, who rekindled the flame of respect for one same among Hindus in proposing and propagating political philosophy for the Hindu Nation.

One minute before ten o'clock, the Secretary of the Court announced the arrival of the Judge. The photographers focused their cameras on the Judge and the dazzling lights blazed and they blinked one after another. Shri CK Daphtary stood up, saluted the judge, and read the charge sheet against the accused and presented it to the Court.

The Court organized the witness statements that would be given to the attorneys defenders on June 2, 1948. The Court would meet again on June 3, 1948. After come back from court, we fix our luggage.

As decided earlier, the Prosecutor's Office provided Shri Annarao Bhopatkar a copy of the witness statements. Even though Shri Bhopatkar advocated for Savarkar, he was entrusted with the general orientation of the defense. Shri Ganpat Rai, Shri Jamnadas Mehta and other defense lawyers assisted the rest of the defendants in addition to working for the defense of Savarkar.

The Court brought the charges against us defendants on June 22, 1948. The The judge asked each of us if we accepted the charges as true; we the we deny. Madan Lal submitted a written statement denying the charges, in which He said:

I deny that there was ever a conspiracy to harm Mahatma Gandhi or that I was involved in said conspiracy. The incident of January 20, 1948 was only intended to show the discontent of the country because of the pro-Muslim policy and the position that Gandhi defended in those days. Nothing else.

While denying the charges, Dr. Parchure claimed to be a resident of Gwalior. The state Gwalior had not acceded to the Union Government of India at the time, and the Government of India had not issued the extradition order against Dr. Parchure before he was taken into custody.

Shri CK Daphtary, Head of the Public Ministry, opened the case and at the end of the day asked the Court to visit the site of the incident. Nathuram declined. Apte, Karkare, Madan Lal and Gopal (myself) indicated our desire to go to the place, while Shankar Kistaiyya, Dr. Parchure and Savarkar said they were not interested. The visit was set at 10 am of June 24, 1948.

We observed the place in order to respond to the statements that the prosecutors could do to prove the charge against us. But that was a minor consideration for us since our attorneys were more competent. He thinking that we were intimately tied to the background to the incident Because the site suddenly came into the open, it dominated our minds.

That was a point at which a chapter in Indian history was closed, for it is where ended the life of one who for decades had dominated the political life of the nation. Was a place where for people of a peaceful spirit it became imperative to risk their lives. It was a place where society, full of blood as a consequence of false notions of the Muslim-Hindu unit, went to show Gandhiji his open wounds and the deep sorrow of their hearts, and to tell him the horrifying stories of the thousands of Partition victims. That was a place where they expected their bleeding sores They will find a voice to communicate their unbearable anguish to the world. But, it was also where the selfish sycophants gathered around Gandhiji to make him believe that his politics nonviolence was completely successful and that the political revolution had without a single drop of blood having been spilled. This was the same place where Gandhiji confirmed to Maulana Azad that the refugees from

Pakistan they had sought asylum in India and who stayed in the homes of Muslims who had left the country to go to Pakistan should be extradited, and who should be convinced to return to the Muslims who left to have their property returned to them. Here he took to held the fast to force the government to reverse its decision to withhold payment of fifty and five tens of million rupees. Finally, it was where the anti-politics policies emanated. Hindu, and as they emerged, in the years to come they were conveniently adopted for paltry profits.

As we saw the place, history was revealed again before our eyes. This recent past was not as clear as they made it see, nor was it placid. We felt that the atmosphere itself was overloaded with blood, the blood of the martyrs who gave their lives in order to achieve national freedom, the blood of the innocent, victims of inhuman atrocities committed due to the vivisection of the country. We also felt that as an intrinsic concomitant to all this, Gandhiji's blood gave it a more deep into this already terrible atmosphere. And now, perhaps as a climactic plan, this dreadful atmosphere thirsty for blood, at least some of us.

All this blood spilled and to be shed was, I think, the price paid for the long-awaited national independence. Her murder was likely to demand sacrifice of the lives of some of us, the accused. While they said that it had been reached Swaraj without any killing, we reluctantly insulted, and sadly we did not give account, the blood so profusely shed of millions of Hindus. We actually were deluded by ladino and selfish politicians and their sycophants, for overwhelming us with this falsehood day after day.

The trial began and the prosecution began with the evidence. The intention of the prosecution was to establish connections between the accused during the period of possible days conspiracy. Nathuram Godse and Narayan Apte were the editor and CEO, respectively, from the Hindu Rashtra newspaper. This data was indisputable. The prosecution showed the trips they took together to Bombay, Delhi and Gwalior. Then he explained his stay at the Hotel Marina, in New Delhi between January 17, 1948 and January 20, 1948 and in the railway station compartment at the Delhi Intersection on 29-30 January 1948.

The prosecution also alleged that Karkare, myself (Gopal Godse), Madan Lal Pahwa, Digambar Badge and Shankar Kistatyya had met at the Marina Hotel on January 1948. But for this accusation there was no evidence other than Digambar Badge, the informer.

A witness from the Hotel Marina, where Nathuram and Apte had stayed, brought his list to show your income under fictitious names.

A taxi driver testified taking us to Nathuram Godse, Narayan Apte, me, Vishnu Karkare, Digamber Badge and Shankar Kistatyya at Birla House on the afternoon of 20 January 1948, and that also brought three of us back to Connaught Place.

The prosecution presented some witnesses to prove that Dr. Parchure was originally from of British India, that is, of the area that was not ruled by the Princes. The prosecution wanted to establish that since Dr. Parchure was from British India, he needed an extradition order. There was still another point. In the Gwalior State there there was the Arms Act. Dr. Parchure could not be charged with a crime under the Act of Weapons if proven to have come from Gwalior, whose status, to the day in question, is not had melted into the Union of India.

In order to show that the conspiracy continued even after January 20, 1948 until the task of assassinating Ganghi Ji was achieved on January 30, 1948, the prosecution brought a witness from Thane (Maharashtra) to prove that there was a meeting between Nathuram Godse, Narayan Apte, Karkare and myself. A simple meeting would not demonstrate the existence of a conspiracy.

The evidence against Veer Savarkar and his rebuttal were later narrated. The prosecution brought 149 witnesses. His evidence ran to 720 pages.

Then, on November 8, 1948, it was the defendants' turn. Not the accused. 1 era Nathuram Vinayak Godse. He wanted to submit a detailed statement. Shri CK Daphtary objected to making a lengthy statement. The Special Judge denied the objection and said, "Go ahead, make your statement." And, Nathuram Godse started with words that resounded.

If You Please, Your Lady:

❏

Part I

Answer to the Charge Sheet

I, Nathuram Vinayak Godse, the first defendant mentioned above, respectfully ask state the following:

1. Before reaching any agreement concerning the various charges, so I respectfully allege that they do not adhere to the law to the extent that there is an association prohibited and there should be two separate trials, one related to the incident of 20 January 1948 and the other with January 30, 1948. It is a vice to have mixed both.

2. Without prejudice to my prior agreement, I do so with respect to the various charges raised and declared hereinafter.

3. On the main charge sheet against the defendants, a number of charges and each suspect is charged both individually and collectively with the commission of various offenses punishable under the Indian Penal Code and other statutes.

4. From the charge sheet it seems that the Prosecutor's Office takes the events that occurred on 20 January 1948 and January 30, 1948 as one and the same or as a chain of events in continuation of an objective that culminated in the death of Gandhiji. By Consequently, I want to make it clear from the outset that the events up to January 20, 1948 are independent and have no connection to what happened after that Nor with what happened on January 30, 1948.

5. The first and foremost charge mentioned is conspiring to assassinate Gandhiji. Therefore I must deal with the same first. I say there was no conspiracy of any kind among the

accused to commit any of the crimes mentioned in the charge sheet. At the same time I declare that I did not instigate any of the other defendants in the committed the crimes alleged.

6. I say that the evidence given by the Prosecutor's Office does not establish or prove that any conspiracy. The only witness who claims about the alleged conspiracy is Digambar R. Badge (Witness 57). He is an unreliable witness as my Attorney, Your Honor, when I explain the evidence in the case and deal with this witness - PW 57.

7. Regarding the charge of collecting and transporting weapons and ammunition without a license, and the complicity of January 20, 1948, I deny the charge and allege that I neither charged nor I transported cotton powder sheets, hand grenades, detonators, fuses, pistols or revolvers, cartridges, etc., nor did I have under my control any of the weapons or ammunition, nor I induced or assisted any of the defendants to do so before, during, or around the 20th January 1948 or any other date. Therefore I deny that I have violated any of the provisions of the Indian Arms Act or Explosive Substances Act and that there is committed any crime punishable under the Acts mentioned.

8. The main evidence regarding this charge is Digambar R. Badge (PW 57), but as stated in paragraph 6, he is an unreliable witness. This witness, Badge (PW 57), he is known to me, but he rarely came with me and I did not visit him in his address for several years. Your declaration of having come to the Rashtra Office Hindu on January 10, 1948, brought by Apte, defendant No. 2, is totally false and I deny that he saw me in the Hindu Rashtra Office or anywhere else that day, or that in my He and Apte's presence will talk about powder cotton sheets, hand grenades, etc. and on the delivery of the same in Bombay. His statement that Apte asked me to leave the fourth and to give him the grenades ... and that a job had been completed is completely false. Badge made up this story to implicate me and the others in the alleged conspiracy.

I certify that I neither saw nor met Badge on January 14, 1948 at Dadar either alone or in the company of Apte. I didn't even know that Badge had come that day to Bombay.

9. I further disbelieve that I was in my possession or under my control, while I was in Delhi, or to induce someone to have and possess arms or ammunition on 20 January 1948 as stated in the charge sheet under the title "Second" paragraphs B (1) and (2).

Again, the evidence supporting this accusation is from Badge only and He asserted that he gave false tests to save his own skin because, only in that condition, it could secure the forgiveness that was promised and granted.

10 Regarding the charge under the title "Third," I deny the charge mentioned and its complicity as stated in various paragraphs A (1) and (2), and B (1) and (2).

11. Regarding the title position "Fourth" paragraph 2, I deny having induced Madanlal K. Pahwa, either by myself or with others, to detonate an iron of cotton powder on January 20, 1948 at the Birla House; there is no evidence to support this accusation, and whatever there might be, I could hardly connect with the explosion.

12. Regarding the charge of conspiracy in the attempt to assassinate Mahatma Gandhi 'under the heading "Fifth" on the charge sheet, I deny it and I assure you that I had no connection either directly or indirectly with Madanlal K. Pahwa or some another person. I say there is no evidence to support this charge.

13. Regarding the position with title "In sixth place" of the charge sheet, paragraphs To (1) and (2) of the same, I express that I did not import or bring pistols without a license or ammunition with help from Narayan D. Apte. I further deny that Dr. Dattatraya S. Parchure and Narayan D. Apte obtained the mentioned pistol or any of them individually or in set; neither was I or they incited to obtain the weapons. Likewise, I declare that the evidence presented by the Prosecutor's Office

is not reliable. Without prejudice to the above, I believe that even if the acts mentioned in paragraphs A (1) and (2) had been committed, this Honorable Court has no jurisdiction to pay attention to them. It worries me that the position be joined with that of paragraph B (1).

14. Regarding the position in paragraph B (1) and (2), I admit that I had in my possession the automatic pistol No. 606824 and its cartridges. Neither Narayan D. Apte nor Vishnu R. Karkare they had nothing to do with the weapon in my possession.

15. But, before taking office under the title "In seventh place", I will not be out of place in explaining how I got to Delhi and why. It's never been a secret the fact that I supported the ideology or the school that was opposed to Gandhiji's. I believe firmly that the teachings of absolute "Ahimsa" defended by Gandhiji in the long run would result in the emasculation of the Hindu Community and thus it would become unable to resist aggression or incursion by other communities, especially Muslims. For to counteract this evil, I resolved to enter public life and formed a group with people whohave a similar perspective. In this, Apte and I take an initiative role, We started with the newspaper "Agrani". It was not so much the Gandhian teachings "Ahimsa" to which my group and I were opposed, but when Gandhiji defended his point of view, always showed or made evident a bias towards Muslims, detrimental to the Hindu Community and its interests. I have described in detail and quoted various examples that undoubtedly establish how Gandhiji was responsible for a countless calamities that the Hindu Community had to suffer and endure.

16. In my journal "Agrani" or "Hindu Rashtra", I always criticized the vision of Gandhiji and his methods such as fasting to achieve his goal, and, after Gandhiji will start holding prayer meetings, we, Apte and I, decided organize peaceful demonstrations to show opposition. We make said

demonstrations in Panchagani, Poona, Bombay, and Delhi. There was a great gulf between both ideologies and grew larger and larger as concessions were made to the Muslims, either at the suggestion or consent of Gandhiji and the Guided Congress by him, culminating in the partition of the country on August 15, 1947. I address this point in detail hereinafter. On January 13, 1948, I learned that Gandhiji had decided continue fasting until death. The reason given for the fast was that he wanted a guarantee of Hindu-Muslim unity in Indian rule. But, both me and others We knew that the real motive behind this was not Hindu-Muslim unity, but force the government to pay the sum of 55 tens of million rupees to Pakistan, payment that he had been emphatically rejected by himself. In response to this, Apte suggested the same method to carry out an energetic but peaceful demonstration in the Gandhiji's prayer meetings. I agreed to this without much enthusiasm, seeing his futility. However, I agreed to join him as no other plan occurred to me. It was for It is for this reason that ND Apte and I went to Bombay on January 14, 1948.

17. On January 15, 1948, we, Apte and I, went in the morning to the Hindu Sabha Office in Dadar. I happened to see Badge there. Seeing us, Badge asked ND Enter the reason for your arrival in Bombay. Apte replied. On your own, Badge offered to come to Delhi and join the rally, if we didn't have any. objection. We wanted men to support us and shout slogans; Thus we accept. We told him when we would start. At that, Badge commented to Apte that he hadto give Pravin Chandra Sethia some things, which he would do in a day or two and see us on January 17, 1948.

18. After meeting Badge on January 15, 1948 in the Office Hindu Sabha, I saw him on January 17, 1948 in the morning.

19. The statements made by Badge about our going with Dixitji Maharaj, about Apte telling him that Savarkar had entrusted us with the task of ending Gandhiji, Pandit Jawaharlal and Surhawardy is pure invention and product of the mind of

Badge. Neither Apte nor I said anything like this to Badge or anyone else. I categorically deny what the Prosecutor's Office has falsely maintained that I was guided in my conduct by Veer Savarkar, and that, were it not for his complicity, I would never I would have acted the way I did. I take the strongest exception to this false e unfair charge which I see as an insult to my intelligence and judgment. The attempt by proving that I was nothing more than someone else's tool is a slander find it far from the truth; in fact, it is a misrepresentation of it.

20. Badge's statement concerning the fact that I wanted to go to Poona to meet my brother Gopal Godse, who had been in charge of making arrangements to obtain a revolver, and bring it to Bombay to accompany us to Delhi, also is a lie. I did not speak to Badge on January 15, 1948, except as stated in paragraph 17. Also, Badge's statement of having met me on January 16, 1948 in Poona it is equally false. The supposed report of my conversation with him in Poona is also false. I was not in Poona on January 16, 1948. It will be clear that it is not true that he given a pistol in exchange for a large revolver on that day.

21. I have already stated that we, Apte and I, had planned to carry out an energetic but peaceful demonstration as early   as possible in the gathering to pray for Gandhiji in Delhi; for that, Apte and I would go there. As stated in paragraph 17, Badge offered to come to Delhi to be part of the aforementioned demonstration previously. We felt an urgent need to bring some volunteers with us to succeed. Before heading to Delhi we started collecting money for pay travel and volunteer expenses.

22. I strongly deny that we saw Savarkar on January 17, 1948 or May He have blessed us with the words "Yashasvi Houn Ya" (Succeed and come back). In the same way, I deny that we talked to Badge or that Apte or I have uttered the words *"Tatyaravani ase Bhavishya kele ahe ki Gandhijichi Shambhar Varshe bharali - ata apale kam nishchita honar yat kahi sanshaya*

nahi. " After what we met Badge on January 15, 1948 at the Hindu Sabha Office in Dadar, we, Apte and I, are continuing our business in relation to the press.

23. Apte and I flew into Delhi on January 17, 1948, and we stayed at the Marina Hotel. On the morning of January 20, 1948, Badge arrived at the hotel and informed Apte in my presence that he and his servant Kistaiya would go to the land of prayer in the afternoon with him just to see the stage where the demonstration would take place. Me I was lying on the bed since I felt unwell due to intense pain from head and I told Badge I might not go. Badge's statements that Apte, Gopal Godse, Karkare, Madanlal, Badge and their servant Shankar met at the Marina hotel; that Shankar and Badge ate there; that Gopal Godse was found repairing the revolver; that Apte, Karkare, Madanlal and Badge went to the bathroom and fixed the detonators, the wire fuses and primers to gunpowder sheets and grenades. hand; or that Shankar and I were standing on either side of the bedroom door are totally false. Badge put in my mouth the words *"Badge, this is our last effort - the work must be accomplished - see to it that everything is properly arranged."* I deny having said such words to Badge that or any other day. As stated Previously, Badge came to the room in the morning and informed me that in the afternoon he would attend to the meeting to pray. That day we had no meeting in my room like Badge He says. As far as I know, Gopal Godse was not even in Delhi. Nobody ordered or fixed in the room no detonators, no wire fuses, no primers to the cotton sheets gunpowder or hand grenades. In fact, there was no such weaponry either with me or with Apte. The vivid description of the distribution of arms and ammunition among the of group and identity theft is a lie. You do not need to discuss the evidence and show the falsehood of all these statements as my lawyer will do so in his office.

24. As I stated earlier, unwell by a severe headache, nor I even went to the land of prayer. Apte returned to the

Marina Hotel around 6:00 pm and informed me that he had given an idea of the meeting and that he would be in a position to take.

Hold the rally in a day or two. After about an hour, we heard a commotion at the meeting place due to an explosion and later we found out about the arrest of a refugee. Apte found it wise to leave Delhi; by Consequently we left. It is not true that I met Badge at the Hindu Sabha Bhavan on January 20, 1948. Several witnesses claimed to see me at Birla House on January 1948, but I firmly argue that they were wrong to say so. I consider that they mistook my presence for someone else's. The identification given by some of these is absolutely unreliable in view of the fact that I was not that day at the Casa Swipe. These witnesses identified me when the Police showed me before them while I was kept at the Tuglak Highway Police Station. Also, it was easy to identify for the bandage that I wore on my head until February 12, 1948. Police witnesses that they deposed before the country they perjured; I raised a complaint from the Delhi witnesses from the first identification round that took place in Bombay.

25. After deliberately analyzing our plan to hold the demonstration at the meeting to pray in Delhi, I reluctantly agreed to accompany Mr. Apte. It was not possible getting capable and willing volunteers from Bombay and Poona under this new situation. On the other hand, our funds were exhausted, we were not in a position enough to spend on bringing a group of volunteers from Bombay to Delhi and then back. We therefore opted to go to Gwalior to see Dr. Parchure who had volunteers from Hindu Rashtra Sena. It was something of an inexpensive alternative to bring volunteers from Gwalior to Delhi. Then we went to Gwalior, on January 27, 1948 we arrived in plane to Delhi, we took the night train that would take us to Gwalior very early in the morning. It was very dark when we stopped at a Dharamshala near the station; in the morning we saw Dr. Parchure at his

residence. I was in a hurry to go to her dispensary. He asked us to see him in the afternoon. We meet him at approximately 4:00 pm and we found out that he did not want to help us and that his volunteers were busy with local affairs. Completely disappointed, I asked I wanted to go back to Bombay or Poona to try to get people there; i came back to Delhi telling him that I myself would try to volunteer among the refugees. I categorically and vehemently deny that Mr. Apte and I went to Gwalior to make us a revolver or a pistol, since these were offered clandestinely. Having reached Delhi in great despair, I visited the refugee camps. As I walked through the fields, my thoughts took a final and decisive turn. I was fortunate to run into a refugee who dealt with weapons and who showed me the gun. I was tempted to have it, so I bought it for him. It is the same one that I used later in the shooting. Returning to the Delhi Railway Station I spent the entire night of the 29th thinking and reflecting on my resolve to end the present chaos and imminent destruction of the Hindus. Now I will discuss in detail my relationship with Veer Savarkar on political and other matters that the accusing party has referred so much to.

26. Born into a devout Brahmin family, I instinctively adopted the religion Hindu, its history and its culture. I have taken pride in Hinduism completely. Not However, as I grew older, I developed a tendency for unfettered free thinking by no superstitious fidelity to any political or religious "ism". That is why I worked actively for the eradication of untouchability and the caste system based exclusively on birth. I publicly joined anti-caste movements and I argued that all Hindus should be treated with the same status as to social and religious rights, and that they should be upper or lower class according to their merits, not by an accident of birth in a particular caste or profession. Used to take part in organize dinners at which thousands of Hindus, Brahmins, Chatria, Vaisyas, Shamares, and Banguis broke caste rules and dined in each other's company.

27. I have read the works of Dadabhai Naoroji, Vivekanand, Gokhale and Tilak along with the ancient and modern history books of India and some countries prominent such as England, France, the United States and Russia. Not only that, also I studied the principles of Socialism and Communism quite well. But above all, I studied very closely what Veer Savarkar and Gandhiji had written and spoken about; to me view, these two ideologies contributed more than any other factor to shape the thought and action of modern India in the last fifty years or less.

28. All these readings and thoughts led me to believe that it was my duty above all to serve Hinduism and the Hindu people, as a patriot and even as humanitarian. Well, isn't it true that ensuring liberty and safeguarding the interests of some thirty tens of millions of Hindus constituted the freedom and well-being of a fifth of the human race? This conviction naturally made me dedicate myself to new Hindu Sangha ideology and programming what only I came to believe could win and preserve the national independence of Hindustan, my motherland and likewise enable you to render true service to humanity.

29. I worked for several years in RSS and subsequently joined the Mahasabha Hindu and volunteered to fight as a soldier under the Pan-Hindu flag. At this time it was chosen Veer Savarkar to the presidency of the Hindu Mahasabha. The Hindu Sangha movement spread and vivified like never before, under his magnetic leadership and propaganda type whirlwind. Millions of Hindu sanghas saw him as the chosen hero, as the defender more capable and faithful of the Hindu cause. I was also one of them. I worked with dedication to go ahead with the activities of the Mahasabha and that is why I came to get acquainted with Savarkarji.

30. Later, my friend and colleague in the Hindu cause, Mr. Apte and I We decided to start a newspaper dedicated to the Hindu Sangha Movement. We met a large number of

prominent Sangha-Hindu leaders and, having gained their sympathy and financial support we met Veer Savarkar as president of the Mahasabha. He too sympathized with our project and advanced us a sum of fifteen thousand rupees as his quota to the required capital on the condition that a limited liability company be registered at our convenience and that your advance will be transformed into large amounts Profits.

31. Consequently, we started the Marathi-speaking daily "Daily Agrani" and after a period a limited liability company was registered. Sums Advances from Veer Savarkar and others were converted into dividends of Rs. 500 each. Among the directors and donors were such important and respected gentlemen as Seth Gulab Chand (brother of Shriman Seth Walchand Hirachandji), Mr. Shingre, a former Bhor's minister, Shreeman Bhalji Pendharkar, the Kolhapur magnate, among others. Mr. Apte and I were the CEOs of the company. I was the editor responsible for the politics of the newspaper. For years we run the newspaper under strict guidelines constitutional laws, and generally uphold Hindu Sangha policy.

32. As representatives of the press of this newspaper, Mr. Apte and I visited the Hindu Sangha Office, located in the central room on the ground floor of Veer's house

Savarkar. This office was under the command of Mr. GV Damle, secretary of Veer Savarkar and Mr. Appa Kasar, his bodyguard. We went to the office to receive from from Mr. Damle, the secretary, public statements issued by Veer Savarkar for the press in general, to record relevant information about the President's trips, interviews, etc. that his secretary was authorized to publish. Mr. AS Bhide, who edited an English weekly called "Free Hindustán" also resided with his family as tenant in a set of rooms on the same ground floor. The second reason why Mr. Apte and I used to visit Savarkar Sadan was to see Messrs Bhide, Damle, Kasar and other Hindu Sabha workers who used to meet at the Hindu Sabha Office and who were friends with us. When we were in Bombay, we went to the office every time we wanted to see them and have friendly talks. Sometimes we discussed the sangha work Hindu with them. Some helped us get advertisements for our newspaper.

33. But, it should be pointed out that these visits to Savarkar Sadan are generally limited to the Hindu Sangha Office, located on the ground floor for the reasons above mentioned. Veer Savarkar resided on the first floor of the house. It was very rare the time We could personally interview Veer Savarkar, and that was by special appointment.

34. About three years ago, Veer Savarkar's health took a serious turn deteriorated and since then she has been confined to bed. After that, he suspended all his public activities and more or less retired from public life. Deprived of his leadership virile and its magnetic influence, the activities and mastery of the Hindu Mahasabha they were also mutilated; and when Dr. Mookerjee became its president, the Mahasabha really was reduced to the position of a maid of Congress. He truly became unable to counter the dangerous activities of the cabal Gandhi on the one hand, and the Muslim League on the other. Seeing this, I lost all hope in the efficiency of the policy of leading the Hindu Sangha movement under the constitutional statutes of the Mahasabha and began to stand up for myself. I committed to organizing a young band of Sangha-Hindus and adopted a program that fought both Congress and the League without consulting any of those prominent but old leaders of the Mahasabha.

35. I must mention here, as one of many surprising examples that painfully opened my eyes at this time to the fact that Veer Savarkar and other old leaders of the Mahasabha were no longer trusted as much to me as to Hindu youth about my persuasion to lead or even to sympathize with the combat program that we hoped would counter with Gandhiji's activities within and with the Muslim League abroad. In or around 1946, the Muslim atrocities perpetrated towards Hindus under the patronage of the Suhrawardy's rule in Noakhali made our blood boil. Our

Shame and outrage knew no boundaries when we saw that Gandhiji protected Suhrawardy and began treating him as "Shahid Saheb—A Martyr Soul" even in his prayer meetings. Not only that, but upon his arrival in Delhi, Gandhiji began to organize his meetings in a Hindu temple and persisted in reading passages from the Qur'an as part of prayer, despite the protest of the Hindu worshipers of the place. Of course I don't know he dared to read the Gita in a mosque in defiance of the Muslim opposition. I knew that of Had he done so, a terrible reaction would have occurred. However, he could stomp without danger the feelings of tolerant Hindus. To contrast with your belief, I determined to prove to him that Hindus can also be intolerant when their honor.

36. Mr. Apte and I decided to hold a series of demonstrations in their meetings in Delhi to make it impossible for him to keep such prayers. Along with a great refugee section, Mr. Apte conducted a procession condemning Gandhi and Shahid Suhrawardy, who rushed to the meeting to pray in the Bhangi Colony. Gandhiji cunningly took refuge behind guarded gates guarded by guards at even though we had no intention of using any force at that time.

37. When Veer Savarkar read the report of the rally, instead of value our move, called me and privately blamed me for such tactics anarchists, even if they were in a peaceful way. Said:

Just as I condemn the congressmen for ending their meetings of party and their polling booths due to disorderly conduct, I must also condemn any undemocratic behavior by part of the Sangha-Hindus. If Gandhiji preached anti-Hindus in your prayer meetings, you should have organized yours to condemn his teachings. All parties should conduct their propaganda under strict constitutional statutes.

38. The second major incident took place after this, when the partition of India was decided. A group of Mahasabha-Hindus wanted to show what his attitude should be with respect to the Government Congress, which would undoubtedly be the Government of the New State, ruling over the so-called Indian

State in the remaining part from the country. Veer Savarkar and other senior mahasabha-Hindu leaders, quickly and energetically said that any government formed to lead a free Indian state It should not be seen as a one-party government, a government of Congress, but rather it was to be honored and obeyed as a National Government of Hindustan; and whatever who deplored the creation of Pakistan, their future motto would be loyal and supreme support for the nascent Indian Free State. Only in this way would it be possible to safeguard the recent Freedom. Any attempt on his part to break the Indian State would provoke a Civil War and would enable Muslims to fulfill their sinful and secret mission of converting all India in Pakistan.

39. Anyway, my friends and I returned unconvinced. We felt in our hearts that the time had come to dismiss Veer Savarkar from the leadership and to stop consulting you on our future policy and program. Neither we should have trusted him with our subsequent plans.

40. Right after that occurred the terrible explosion of Muslim fanaticism in the Punjab and other parts of India. The congressional government began to persecute, prosecute and shoot Hindus who dared to resist Muslim forces in Bihar, Calcutta, Punjab, among others. Our worst fears seemed to come true; and without However, how painful and regrettable it was for us to learn that it was celebrated on August 1947 with lighting and festivities, while all of Punjab was ablaze and rivers of Hindu blood flowed. The sympathetic Mahasabha-Hindus decided to boycott the celebrations of the Congressional Government and launch an action program that will control Muslim violent attacks.

41. The meetings of the Hindu Mahasabha Working Committee and the Convention All India Hindu were held on August 9-10, 1947, in Delhi, Veer Savarkar presided. Mr. Apte, other friends and I wanted to make one last attempt to attract the Mahasabha and its veteran leaders such as Veer Savarkar,

Dr. Mookerjee, Mr. LB Bhopatkar, and others towards our vision and adopt an offensive resolution. He Mahasabha Working Committee did not accept our suggestion to appoint a council of action against Haiderabad or to boycott the Congressional Government that was the newly created State of Divided India. For me, to recognize a state of the Divided India was tantamount to being a supporter of the cursed vivisection of the country. Instead, the Working Committee passed an empty resolution and asked people to hoist in their homes the flag of Bhagwa on August 15, 1947. Veer Savarkar went further and truly insisted that the tricolor flag with the wheel should be recognized as the Flag National. We openly take his attitude the wrong way.

42. Not only that but, on August 15, putting aside the desire of the majority of the Sangha-Hindus, at his home together with the Bhagwa, Veer Savarkar raised this new flag with the wheel as National Flag. Furthermore, when Dr. Mookerji, through from a long distance phone call, asked your permission as to whether to accept a portfolio in the Indian Union Ministry, Veer Savarkar answered sharply that the new Government should be recognized as a National Government regardless of the party elected to govern it, and that it should be supported by all patriots, and consequently, Sangha-Hindus should cooperate by accepting a portfolio if instructed to do so. To its Once, he congratulated the Ministers of Congress for the attitude of commitment they were taking on calling a Hindu-Sabha leader like Dr. Mookerji to participate in the formation of the National Ministry. Mr. Bhopatkar also supported Dr. Mookerji.

43. By this time it came to light that some of the top leaders of the Congress and some of the Province Ministers had also contacted Veer Savarkar and that there was an active correspondence between them to form a united front in support for the new state, whose policy Veer Savarkar had already defended. I myself do not could oppose a common front of patriots, but while the Congress of the Government

continued to be timidly under the yoke of Gandhiji and while he was able to give push their anti-Hindu fashions to the Congressional Government by resorting to such a simple trick like the threat of a hunger strike, it was more than clear to me than any front common under such circumstances was bound to be another way to establish the Dictatorship of Gandhji, and as a consequence, a betrayal of Hindudom.

44. He resented each of these steps taken by Veer Savarkar so much that, Together with Mr. Apte and some of the young Sangha-Hindu friends we decided, once and for all, design and develop our active program very independent of the Mahasabha or their old leaders. We agree not to trust any of our new plans to anyone, including Veer Savarkar.

45. I began to criticize the Hindu Mahasabha and the politics of its old leaders in my diary "Agrani" or "Hindu Rashtra" and to openly call the young generation of sangha-Hindus to accept our active program.

46. To develop my new independent plan, I decided to undertake two matters with which to start. The first was to undertake a series of powerful but peaceful demonstrations against Gandhiji to make him feel the impact of Hindu discontent organized, and create confusion and disorder through demonstrative protests, etc. in their hateful prayer meetings, although afterwards he carried out his anti-Hindu propaganda; and in second, to carry out a campaign against the Haiderabad State to defend our Hindu brothers and sisters near the border line of atrocities by fanaticism that Muslims committed against them. Since such a program could only be carried out under secret and dictatorial guidelines, we resolved to disclose it only to Those who believed in him and who would obey our orders without question.

47. I would not have referred to the previous details in this statement had it not been for the opening speech of the tax attorney in which he portrayed me as a vile tool in Veer Savarkar's hands. I felt that such a statement had

been a deliberate insult to my freedom of judgment and action. I should have mentioned the above facts to dispel the impression wrong towards me, if anything. Therefore, before I expose the rest of my statement, I again assert that it is not true that Veer Savarkar was aware of my activities that finally led me to shoot Gandhiji, I repeat that is not true and that it is completely false that Mr. Apte in my presence or I have told him to Badge that Veer Savarkar had given us the order to finish off Gandhiji, Nehru and Suhrawardy, as the whistleblower has falsely alleged. It is not true that ever we will take Badge to Veer Savarkar's house to take the last Darshan in relation with such a plot or that Veer Savarkar told us: "Yashasvi houn ya" (Succeed and come back). Neither Mr. Apte nor I told Badge that Veer Savarakar had commented that the hundred years of Gandhiji had ended and that we were therefore destined to be successful. I was not even superstitious enough to beg for such blessings nor childish enough to believe such divinations.

❏

Part II

Gandhiji Policies Unraveled

Section I

48. The atmosphere prior to the event of January 30, 1948 was complete and exclusively political and I would like to explain it later. The fact that Gandhiji honor the holy books of Hindus, Muslims, and others, or that during their prayers reciting verses from the Gita, the Koran and the Bible never provoked animosity in me towards his person. For me, studying religion is not objectionable comparative. It is a merit indeed.

49. The territory comprised by the Northwest Border to the north and the Cape Comorin to the south and the areas between Karachi and Assam is pre-departure India which has always been for me my mother country. In this vast land, people of various religions and I hold that these creeds should have full and equal freedom to follow their ideals and beliefs. In this area, the Hindus are the most numerous. They have nowhere else the which they can call their own beyond or outside this country. Therefore, since time immemorial, Hindustan is for Hindus both the mother country and the holy land. This territory must to the Hindus their fame and their glory, their culture and their art, their knowledge, science and philosophy. After the Hindus, the Muslims are numerically predominant. Since the ... century X have made systematic advances in the territory and gradually succeeded in establishing the Islam in most of India.

50. Before the arrival of the British, both Hindu and Muslim, for The result of centuries of experience, they had realized that Muslims could not remain like the masters in India nor be chased away. They were clear that they were both here to stay. Due to the rise of the Maharattas, the revolt of the rajputs and the uprising of the Sikhs, Muslims claimed that the country had weakened, and although some of them still aspired to supremacy in India, the people practice could clearly see that such hopes were futile. On the other hand, British had proven to be more powerful than Hindus and Muslims in battle and intrigue, and by its adoption of improved methods of administration and guarantee from security to life and property without any discrimination, both Hindus and Muslims accepted them. Differences between Hindus and Muslims existed even before for the British to arrive. However, it is a reality that the British made the increased unscrupulous use of these differences and created even more to retain their power and authority. The Indian National Congress, created with the objective of acquiring power for the people in the government of the country, had from the beginning upheld the ideal of a complete nationalism which implied that all Indians should enjoy the same rights and total equality as the foundation of democracy. This ideal of removing a external government and replace it with democratic power and the authority of the people called my attention from the beginning of my public career. 51. In my writings and speeches I have always defended that the considerations religious and communal should be avoided in the public affairs of the country, in elections, inside and outside the legislatures and in the realization and dissolution of the Cabinets. From the In principle I have advocated a secular state with a mixed electorate; for me it's the only thing reasonable to do. (Here I read excerpts from the resolutions transmitted in the Session Bilaspur of Hindu Mahasabha in December 1944. Pages 12 and 13 annexed). Under the influence of Congress, this ideal was progressing steadily among the Hindus. But Muslims,

as a community, initially held out margin, and later, under the corrosive influence of the Divide and Conquer Policy of the foreign teachers, they wanted to foster the ambition to dominate the Hindus. The first Indicator of this vein was the demand for a separate electorate instigated by the then Viceroy Lord Minto in 1906. The British Government acceded to this demand with the excuse of protection of the minority. While the Congress Party offered an opposition of verbally, he progressively supported separatism by finally adopting the formula notorious for neither accepting nor rejecting it in 1934.

52. Consequently, it originated and intensified the demand for the disintegration of the country. What was at first the thin end of the wedge eventually became Pakistan. However, the mistake began with the laudable project of bringing a united front of all classes of India to expel foreigners, and separatism was expected to would eventually disappear.

53. Despite my support from initially mixed constituencies, I reconsidered the temporary introduction of separate electorates as Muslims were very interested in it. However, I insisted that representation should be strictly guaranteed proportion to the number of each community and no more. I have firmly held this position.

54. Inspired in part by our British masters and by the endorsement of Congress under the leadership of Gandhiji on the other, the Muslim League continued increasing their demands on a community basis. The Muslim community continuously he backed the Muslim League; each subsequent election proved that the League had the fanaticism and ignorance of the Muslim masses and in this way the League was fostered, in its policy of separatism on a scale that increased year by year.

55. As I have stated above, despite your objection regarding the principle of the communal electorate, the unreasonable demands of the Muslim League were granted first by Congress and the Lucknow Pact in 1916, and after that in each successive revision of the constitution. This lapse, of nationalism and

democracy on the part of Congress, has demonstrated a costly calamity as shown by the aftermath.

56. Since 1920, that is, after the death of Lokamanaya Tilak, the Gandhiji's influence in Congress first increased and then became supreme. Their Awakening activities were phenomenal in intensity and were reinforced with the slogan of truth and non-violence, which he ostentatiously flaunted before the country. Not there was a reasonable or brilliant person who could object to these slogans. Not really there was nothing new or original about them. They are implicit in all public movement constitutional. Imagine that the majority of humanity is or may become capable of Scrupulously adhering to these noble principles in your normal day-to-day life is merely a dream. In fact, honoring, committing, and loving one's relatives, friends and the country can make us ignore nonviolence and employ force. He could never conceive that an armed resistance against aggression is unjust. I would consider it a religious and moral duty to resist, if not to defeat, an enemy similar through the use of force. Shree Ramchandra killed Ravan in a fight tumultuous and reassured Sita. Shree Krishna murdered Kansa to end his wickedness. At the Mahabharat, Arjun had to fight and kill a large number of his friends and relatives, including the revered Bhishma because he was on the side of the aggressor. Is my firm belief that treating Rama, Krishna and Arjuna as guilty of violence is revealing a complete ignorance of man's engine of action. It was the heroic fight sustained by Chhatrapati Shivaji Maharaj which first contained and later ended the Muslim tyranny in India. It was a completely correct tactic to assassinate Afzul Khan since otherwise it would have killed him. By condemning Shivaji, Rana Pratap already Guru Govind as misguided patriots, Gandhiji only exposed his conceit.

57. Each one of today's heroes resisted attacks in our country, protected the people against the atrocities and rapes of foreign fanatics and recovered the motherland from the hands

of the invader. On the other hand, during the undisputed leadership of the Mahatma over thirty years there was more desecration of temples, more conversions fraudulent and forced, more rapes of women, and finally the loss of a third part of the territory. That is why it is amazing that his followers cannot see what it is more than evident even to the blind, for example, that the Mahatma was a mere Pygmy compared to Shivaji, Rana Pratap and Guru Govind. Your condemnation of these illustrious heroes was, to say the least, most pretentious.

58. The clique that came to power under the patronage of imperialism British, due to a cowardly surrender to the Partition of India at the point of Muslim violence, now tries to exploit Gandhiji's death in hundreds of ways frantic for their own selfish ends. But history will give them their rightful place in the niche of fame. Gandhiji was, paradoxically, a violent pacifist who brought the country unspeakable calamities in the name of truth and non-violence; while frog Pratap, Shivaji and the Guru will be forever enshrined in the hearts of their compatriots for the freedom they brought them.

59. As noted below in this document, the political activities of Gandhiji can be divided into three sections. He returned to India from England in late 1914 and he immersed himself almost immediately in the political life of the country. Unfortunately little after their arrival, Sir Pherozeshah Mehta and Mr. GK Gokhale, the latter whom Gandhiji called Guru, they died in a short period of time. Gandhiji began his work by starting an Ashram in Ahmedabad on the banks of the Sabarmati River, and did Truth and non-violence their slogans. He himself has admitted that he has often acted against his professed principles and that if it was to appease Muslims, he hardly had any scruples in doing so. Truth and non-violence are excellent as ideal and admirable as guides in action. They are, however, to be practiced in daily life and not in the air. I will show later that Gandhiji was guilty of blatantly breaching his ideals that he boasted so much.

60. Gandhiji's political career will be divided, as already stated, into three aspects:

   (i) The period between 1915 and 1939-40.

  (ii) The period from 1939-40 to June 3, 1947, when Congress Indian National surrendered to Mr. Jinnah and accepted Pakistan under the Mahatma leadership.

 (iii) The period between the date of the partition until the day of its last fast to death which resulted in the payment of 55 tens of million rupees, and the death of the Mahatma in a short time.

61. When Gandhiji finally returned to India in late 1914, he brought with him a very high reputation for the courageous leadership of the Indians in South Africa. He placed himself himself at the head of the struggle for the assertion and vindication of national respect for the India and for our citizenship right against white tyranny in that country. Was honored and obeyed by Hindus, Muslims and Parsis alike and was universally acclaimed as the leader of all Indians in South Africa. His simplicity before life, his devotion altruistic towards the cause which he had made his own, his sacrifice and seriousness in fighting against The racial arrogance of the Afrikaners raised the prestige of the Indians. He had given himself to love by everyone in India.

62. When he returned here to serve his compatriots in their fight for the freedom, legitimately hoped, as in Africa, to command without question the trust and the respect of all communities. He was soon disappointed. India was not South Africa. In South Africa, the Indians asked for nothing more than their elementary rights of citizenship. which were denied them. They all had a common and serious grievance. Boers and British had treated them like rugs. Hence, Hindus, Muslims, and Parsis held together as one against the common enemy. They had no other lawsuit against the South African Government. The problem at home was quite different.

We fought to rule ourselves and even for Independence. We had intent to bring down an Imperial Power, which had entrenched itself in the ground and he was determined to continue his influence on us by all possible means, including the "Divide and Conquer" policy that had intensified the split between Hindus and Muslims. Gandhiji had to face from the beginning a problem of a a kind he had never experienced in South Africa. In fact, in South Africa, everything went In a simple way. The identity of interest between the various communities was complete and every Indian had lined up behind him. But in India, the communal franchise, the separate electorate and dislike had undermined the nation's solidarity, much of it This was seen for leagues and the British continued with the sinister policy of favoritism communal with the utmost tenacity and without any scruples. By this, Gandhiji found extremely difficult to obtain the unquestionable leadership of the Hindus and Muslims as in South Africa. But, he was used to being the leader of all Indians, and frankly, he couldn't understand leadership in a divided country. It was absurd for her honestly think about accepting the strategy of an army divided against itself.

63. For the first five years since his return, there was not much scope for his mission of obtaining supreme leadership in Indian politics. Dadabhai Naoroji, Sir Pherozeshah Mehta, Lokmanya Tilak and Mr. GK Gokhale, among others still were alive, and as much as Gandhiji was honored, and as popular as he was, he was still a rookie compared to veterans in both age and experience. But in a span of five years, an inexorable fate removed them all, and with the death of Lokmanya Tilak in August 1920, Gandhiji was placed in the front row.

64. He realized that with the policy "Divide and conquer", the rulers foreigners corrupted the patriotism of Muslims and that it had minimal opportunity to lead a united army fighting for freedom unless capable of instilling sympathy and common devotion towards the mother country. That is why

he made the Hindu-Muslim unity the foundation of its policy. In response to tactics British, began to reach out to the Muslim community amicably and reinforced these actions by making generous and extravagant promises. This, of course, was not wrong, as long as it was done in a manner consistent with India's fight for national democratic freedom; but Gandhiji forgot it completely, the essential aspect of his campaign for unity, the results of which we now all know.

65. Our British rulers were able, often through Indian resources, to make concessions to Muslims, and to support the various divided communities. By 1919, Gandhiji was desperate in his attempts to get Muslims trusted him and he went from one absurd promise to another. He promised them "a blank check". He supported the Khilafat movement in this country and managed to get the full support of the National Congress in this policy. For a time, Gandhiji seemed to triumph and prominent Muslim leaders from all over India became his followers; Mr. Jinnah does not was nowhere in 1920-21 and the Ali brothers became leaders Muslims. Gandhiji welcomed this as the fulfillment of the promise of leadership towards the Muslims. He made more of the Ali brothers, raised them to the clouds with praise and endless concessions; But what he wanted never happened Muslims led the Khilafat Committee as a distinct political-religious organization and all the time it maintained as a separate entity from Congress; very soon the Moplah Rebellion evidenced that Muslims had no idea of national unity, like Gandhiji he had assumed and had gambled so much. Hence followed, as is usual in such cases, a massive slaughter of Hindus, numerous forced conversions, rapes and arson provoked. The British Government, totally immovable by the rebellion, suppressed it in few months and left Gandhiji the joy of his Hindu-Muslim unity. Agitation Khilafat had failed and disappointed Gandhiji. British Imperialism emerged more strong, the Muslims became more fanatical and the consequences fell on the Hindus. Undaunted by the tactics of

the British rulers, Gandhiji was more stubborn in the search for the ghost of his Hindu-Muslim unity. Thanks to the 1919 Act, the Separate constituencies expanded and communal representation continued not only in the legislature and local entities, but even the Cabinet. Services started distributed according to communal bases and Muslims obtained the best positions on the part of our British teachers, not because of merit, but because of standing margin of the fight for freedom and for being followers of Islam. Government sponsorship to Muslims in the name of minority protection penetrated the entire body of the state policy, and the Mahatma's nonsensical slogans were no match for all this wholesale corruption of the Muslim mindset. However, Gandhiji did not give in. He still lived in hopes of being the common leader for both Hindus and Muslims, and each time he was defeated, he agreed to motivate Muslims by extravagant methods. The position continued to deteriorate and by 1925, It became clear to everyone that the Government had won all along; but how Proverbial gamer, Gandhiji upped the ante. He agreed to the separation from Sind and to the creation of a separate province on the northwestern border. It also granted the League Muslim one undemocratic demand after another in the vain hope of having his support in the national struggle. By this time, the capital of the Ali brothers had exhausted, and Mr. Jinnah, who had prepared his return, had the best of both worlds. Whatever concession the Government or Congress makes, Mr. Jinnah will accepted and asked for more. The separation of Sind from Bombay and the creation of the province of Northwest border were followed by the Round Table Conference where they raised the questions of the minority. Mr. Jinnah stood firm against the federation until Gandhiji himself asked Mr. McDonald, Chairman of the Board of the Work, which will award him the Community Award. In this way seeds were sown that would disintegrate the country. Communal principles were embedded in the Reforms of 1935. The Mr. Jinnah took the greatest advantage of every situation. The Federation of India, made to consolidate the character of the nation, it was in effect defeated. Mr. Jinnah never took it from The best way. Congress continued to support the Community Award under words rather hypocritical of neither support nor rejection, which was actually his acceptance tactic. During the war, 1939-44, Mr. Jinnah adopted an open attitude, a certain neutrality benevolent, and promised to support the war as soon as Muslim rights were granted; In April 1940, after six months of war, Mr. Jinnah appeared with the demand for Pakistan as the basis for his two-nation theory. Mr. Jinnah totally ignored the fact that there were large numbers of Hindus and Muslims in every corner of India. There may be a majority of Hindus and a minority of Muslims in certain provinces and vice versa, but there was no province in India in which there was a negligible amount whether of Hindus or Muslims; a split would leave the minority in question totally helpless.

66. The British Government liked the Pakistani idea as it would keep the Hindus and Muslims alienated during the war and thus prevent shame the government. Muslims did not obstruct the war effort, and the Congress was at times neutral and at other times opposed. On the other hand, the Sabha Hindu realized that this was an opportunity for our young people to have military training, absolutely essential to our nation, of which the British they were intentionally pushing us away. But because of this war, the gates of the Navy, Navy and Air Force, and Mahasabha urged our compatriots to militarize Hindus. The result was that about half a million Hindus learned the art of warfare and mastered the mechanized aspects of warfare modern. Governments in Congress enjoy the fruits of the precautions of the Mahasabha because the troops that they use in Kashmir and that they have employed in Haiderabad they would have been there had it not been for the efforts of men with such a perspective. In In 1942, Congress started the "Leave India" movement in the name of freedom. Congressmen from

all the provinces carried out violent attacks. In the province of Northern Bihar, there was hardly a railway station that had not been burned or destroyed by non-cooperators in Congress; but despite all the opposition from Congress, the Germans were defeated in April 1945, and the Japanese in August 1945. same year. The atomic bomb collapsed the Japanese resistance and the British defeated Japanese and Germans despite opposition from the Congress party. The bell 1942 "Abandon India" had completely failed. The British had triumphed and Congress leaders decided to reach an agreement with them. Actually in the years Following, the policy of Congress could be described as *"Peace at any price"* and *"Congress in office at any cost."* Congress pledged to the British who put him in charge, and instead he surrendered to Mr. Jinnah's violence, who gave him a third of India, an explicitly racial and theological state, and destroyed two million human beings in the process. Pandit Nehru now professes one and again that Congress represents a secular state and violently denounces those who reminded him that just last year he agreed with a Communal and theological state; their vociferous adherence to a *"Secular State"* is nothing Except for one case of *"my wife complains too much."*

67. The "Abandon India" movement had to be abandoned, it had to be ensured Congressional support for the war against Japan and accept Viceroy Lord Wavell as head of the Government of India before Congress was called to the House of Conference.

68 This section summarizes the history of agony over the partition of India and the tragedy of the assassination of Gandhiji. Neither one nor the other gives me pleasure to register or remember, but the Indians and the whole world must know the history of the last thirty years during which the imperialist policy of the British and the misguided policy of communal unity tore India to pieces. The Mahatma had been tricked into act which did not lead to Hindu-Muslim unity, but to the destruction of the base of is. Five tens of millions of

Indian Muslims were no longer ours compatriots; the virtual non-Muslim minority of West Pakistan had been liquidated either by the most brutal murders or by the tragic forced eviction from their lands that they were his from centuries ago; the same process is furiously underway in East Pakistan. One hundred and ten million people had been dispossessed of their homes, of whom no less than four million were Muslims, and when I found out that still After these terrible results, Gandhhiji continued to maintain the same policy of appeasement, my blood boiled, and I couldn't take it anymore. I do not intend to use words high-sounding towards the person of Gandhiji nor hold my opinion of disapproval of him rationale for its policy and methods. Actually, Gandhiji succeeded in doing what the British had always wanted in the execution of their "Divide and Rule" policy. He helped them divide the country and it is not yet certain that his rule has ended.

Gandhiji Policies Unraveled

Section II

69. The accumulated provocation of 32 years culminating in his last fast pro-Muslim, in the end I was led to the conclusion that Gandhiji's existence must come to an immediate end. Upon returning to India he developed a subjective mindset in which only he was the judge of what was right or wrong. If the country wanted his leadership, it had to accept his infallibility, otherwise he would stay away from Congress and continue his own way. Faced with such an attitude there could be no half measures, or Congress would double the hands and was content to play a secondary role in the face of all his eccentricity, his whims, his metaphysics and primitive vision, or she would have to go on without him. Only he was the judge of everything and everyone; he was the mastermind guiding the movement of civil disobedience; nobody else knew his technique; only he knew when to start it and when to remove

it. The movement can succeed or fail; can lead to disasters unspeakable and political defeats, but that would not change the infallibility of the Mahatma. "A Satyagrahi can never fail "was his formula for declaring his own infallibility; and no one Except he knew what a Satyagrahi was. This is how Gandhiji became the judge and your own case lawyer. These inanities and obstinacies that were coupled to a life austere, tireless work and sublime character made Gandhiji formidable and irresistible. Many thought his policies were irrational, but had to decide between retiring of Congress or put his intelligence at his feet to do whatever he wanted with she. With a posture of utter irresponsibility, Gandhiji was guilty of wrongdoing after mistake, failure after failure and disaster after disaster. Not one can be credited political victory in its 33 years of dominance. Later in this document I mention with certain details the amount of blunders he committed during the 32 years of his leadership undisputed.

70. Now I will briefly describe the enormous shenanigans made by the slogans and panaceas that Gandhiji prescribed and followed in pursuance of his policy whose results today we all know. Here are some of them:

(a) **Khilafat**— As a consequence of World War I, Turkey it lost most of its empire in Africa and the Middle East. He also lost all his imperial possessions in Europe and by 1914 only a strip of it remained in the European continent. The young Turks forced the Sultan to abdicate; with the disappearance of this one, the Khilafat was also abolished. The devotion of Indian Muslims to the Khilafat She was strong and serious, and they believed that it was the British who caused the fall of the Sultan and the Khilafat. So they started a campaign for the resurgence of the Khilafat. In an outrage of opportunism, the Mahatma misinterpreted the idea that helping the Khilafat movement would become the leader of Muslims in India, as it was for the Hindus, and that once Hindu-Muslim unity was achieved, the British they would have to concede Swaraj. But again, Gandhiji miscalculated and in guiding Congress National Indian to identify himself with the Khilafat Movement, practically gratuitously introduced the theological element that resulted in a tragic calamity and expensive. For a moment, the Khilafat revival movement seemed to be successful. Muslims who were not with the Khilafat Movement soon came out of the picture and the Ali brothers, who were the leading foremen, climbed to the top of the popularity and conquered it all. For a few years, Mr. Jinnah was a lonely figure which was not taken into account. However, the movement failed. Our British sovereigns were unfazed in the least, and as a combined result of the repression with the Montague Chelmsford Reforms, were able to help the Khilafat movement a few years later. The Muslims supported the Movement Khilafat separated from Congress all the time; they received their support, but they did not mix. When failure came, the Muslims despaired and disappointed, and their anger he punished the Hindus. Countless riots followed in various parts of India. In all sides, most of the victims were Hindus. The Hindu-Muslim unity of the Mahatma a mirage returned.

(b) **Moplah Rebellion**—Malabar, Punjab, Bengal and NWF Province were the scene of repeated attacks against Hindus. The Moplah Rebellion, as you called, was the longest and most concentrated attack against the Hindu religion, its honor, his life and his property; hundreds of Hindus were forcibly converted to Islam; I know they raped women. The Mahatma who had brought all this calamity to India by his Communal politics was kept quiet. He never uttered a single word of reproach in against the aggressors nor did it allow

Congress to take action on the matter with what it would have prevented the repetition of these attacks. On the other hand, he went to the limit of denying the numerous cases of forced conversions in Malabar and even published in his diary "Young India" that there was only one case of forced conversion. Your own colleagues Muslims informed him that he was in error and that forced conversions they abounded in Malabar. He never corrected his misstatements, but went to the extreme absurd to start a relief fund for the Moplahs instead of their victims; Yet there were no signs of the promised land of Hindu unity. Muslim.

(c) **Intrigue Amir Afghan** — When the Khilafat movement failed, the Alí brothers decided to do something that could keep Khilafat feelings with lifetime. His slogan was that anyone who was an enemy of the Khalifat was also an enemy of the Islam, and since the British were primarily responsible for the defeat and dethronement of the Sultan of Turkey, every faithful Muslim had a solemn duty to be an enemy staunch of Great Britain. To that end, they invited the Amir of Afghanistan to invaded India and was promised full support. There is a long story behind this intrigue; the Ali brothers never denied their involvement in the conspiracy. The mahatma continued in his tactics of forming Hindu-Muslim unity by supporting the brothers Ali across the length and breadth. He showed them his affection publicly and promised unconditional support in the restoration of the Khalifat. Even watching the invasion of the Amir in India, the Mahatma directly and indirectly helped the Ali brothers. This is found beyond mere suspicion. The late Mr. Shastri, Mr. CY Chintamani, editor of the "Leader" of Allahabad, and even the Mahatma's longtime friend, the late Rev. CF Andrews told him clearly that his speeches and writings amounted to support towards the Ali brothers in their invitation to the Amir of Afghanistan to invade the India. The following quote from the Mahatma's writing in those days should make it clear that he had forgotten his own nation in his desire to satisfy the Muslims and to had become a supporter of the invasion of a foreign ruler to his mother homeland. The Mahatma supported the invasion with the following words:

I do not understand why they are going to arrest the Ali brothers as the rumors, and why I stay free. They haven't done anything that I haven't would do. If they had texted Amir, I would have too made to inform him that if he came, no Indian could prevent him from helping to the Government to make it roll back.

British surveillance put an end to the conspiracy, nothing came to light of the grotesque plot by the Ali brothers regarding the invasion of India, and the unity Hindu-Muslim remained as distant as before.

(d) (i) **Attack on Arya Samaj**—Gandhiji ostentatiously displayed his love for Muslims through a most undignified and unprovoked attack on the Arya Samaj in 1924. He publicly denounced the Samaj for alleged sins of omission and commission; it was an absolutely unjustified, reckless and unworthy attack; but any one thing that pleased the Mohammedans was their heartfelt desire. The Arya Samaj elaborated a powerful but courteous report, and for some time Gandhiji was silenced, nonetheless the The latter's growing political influence weakened the Arya Samaj. No follower of Swami Dayanand could be a Gandhian Congressman. The two are totally incompatible; But the lure of the position and leadership has led many Arya Samajistas to participate in the double game by calling themselves Gandhian

Congressmen and Arya Samajistas at the same time. The result was that the Government of Sindh imposed a ban on Satyartha Prakash four years ago; Arya Samaj took it with his head lowered. How As a result, their influence on the social and religious life of Hindus has been limited considerably. Individual members of the Samaj are and were strong nationalists. The late Lala Rajpat Lai and Swami Shradhanand, to mention just two names, were unconditional Arya Samajistas, but firstly they were part of the leaders of the Congress until the end of their lives. They did not represent blind support for Gandhiji, but they definitely opposed his pro-Muslim policy, and openly fought against this respect. However, these great men are gone. We know that the Most of the Arya Samaj is still what it was, but is misinformed by the section selfish of the Samaj who guides him in a bad way. The Samaj is no longer the force and the power that once was.

(d) (ii) Gandhiji's attack did not increase his popularity with Muslims, but which caused his youth to kill Swami Shradhanandji a few months later. The charge against the Samaj claiming that it was a reactionary body was manifestly false. Everyone knew that far from being a retrograde organism, the Samaj had been the vanguard of social reforms among the Hindus. For hundreds of years, long before Gandhji was born, the Samaj had advocated the abolition of untouchability. The Samaj had popularized the second marriage for widows. He denounced the caste system and advocated for the unity not only of the Hindus, but of all those who were prepared to follow its principles. For a time Gandhiji was completely silenced, but his leadership made people forget his baseless attack on the Arya Samaj and It even greatly weakened him. Swami Dayanand Saraswati, founder of the Arya Samaj, it did not establish any law on violence or non-violence. In his teachings, I don't know excluded the use of force, but was permissible if it was morally desirable. It must have been a dilemma for the Arya Samaj leaders to decide whether to remain or not in Congress, since Gandhiji insisted on non-violence in all cases and Swami Dayanand did nothing about it. However, Swami died and the popularity of Gandhiji catapulted like a star into the sky.

(e) **Sind Separation** — By 1928, Mr. Jinnah's capital had grown enough and the Mahatma had already granted many of his unfair and improper demands to at the expense of Indian democracy, the nation and Hindus. The Mahatma even supported the separation from Sindh since the Bombay presidency, driving Hindus out of that region towards community wolves. Numerous riots took place in Sind, Karachi, Sukkur, Shikarpur, and other places where only Hindus were the victims; and the Hindu-Muslim unity was increasingly fading over the horizon.

(f) **League bids farewell to Congress** — With each defeat, Gandhiji had more interest in his method of achieving Hindu-Muslim unity. Just like a gambler who He has lost a lot, got desperate, raised the stakes and gave free rein to the more irrational concessions if they could only appease. Mr. Jinnah had the support of the Mahatma's leadership in the fight for freedom. But the distant attitude of the Congressional Muslims grew over the years, and the Muslim League refused to have something to do with Congress after 1928. The Independence resolution passed by Congress at its

Lahore Session in 1929 found that Muslims They stood out for their absence and for being far removed from the organization of Congress. After that, hardly anyone held out hope for Hindu-Muslim unity; even so, Gandhiji remained blindly optimistic and gave himself more and more to the communal system Muslim.

(g) **Round table conference and Community Award—** The authorities British, both in India and England, found that the demand for larger and true deliveries of constitutional reforms was becoming more insistent and with greater fervor in India; and that despite its unscrupulous policy of "Divide and governs "and the community discord that it had generated, the resulting situation did not had given neither the permanence nor the security that the British Government in India had contemplated. Therefore, at the end of 1929 they decided to convene a table conference round in England early the following year and make a statement to that effect. Mr. Ramsay McDonald was Prime Minister and a Government of Labor was in the power; but the action came too late. A month later, despite the declaration mentioned above, the Independence resolution was approved at the Lahore Session Congress, and the Congress Party decided to boycott this Table Conference round. Instead, after a few months, the Salt Campaign began, which created tremendous enthusiasm and nearly 70,000 people went to jails for breaking the provisions of the Salt Act. However, Congress soon regretted its boycott in the First Roundtable Conference, and the 1931 Karachi Congress opted for to send Gandhiji only as a representative of Congress to the Second Conference of round table. Whoever reads the proceedings of that Session will realize that Gandhiji was the main factor in causing the total failure of the Conference. None of

The decisions of the roundtable conference was in support of democracy or nationalism; and the Mahatma went so far as to invite Mr. Ramsay McDonald to grant the so-called Community Prize, in this way reinforced the disintegrating forces of the communal system which had already corroded the political body for 24 years. He Mahatma was thus responsible for the direct and substantial intrusion of the communal electorate and the communal franchise in the future Parliament of India. It is no wonder that when the Mr. Ramsay McDonald presented the Community Award, the Mahatma refused to object and Assembly members were asked to "not support or reject it." the same Gandhiji placed an ax on the communal unit he had wagered so much for during the last fifteen years. Nor is it surprising that under the pretext of protection of the minority, we would place in the Government of India Act of 1935 an acknowledgment permanent statutory of communal franchise, communal electorate and even weight for the minorities, especially Muslims, both in the Provinces and in the Center. Those chosen in the communal franchise would naturally possess that mindset and not would have any interest in bridging the gulf between the communal system and the nationalism. For this reason it was impossible to form a parliamentary party with fundamentals political and economic. Hindus and Muslims divided into opposite camps and they worked as rival parties, giving a growing impetus to separatism. In almost all On both sides, the Hindus became victims of communal orgies at the hands of the Muslims. People had become completely cynical about any possibility of union between Hindus and Muslims, but Gandhiji kept repeating his fruitless formula all the weather. (Here I refer to Pandit Madan Mohan Malaviya's speech against accept the Community Award).

(h) **Approval of charges and resignation in a show of courage** — The Provincial Autonomy since April 1, 1937 under the Government of India Act of 1935. The act was full of privileges, special powers, protection of interests granted and the continuity of the current British staff in the various services to be treated. By That is why Congress did not accept charges at first, but soon realized that in each Province elected a Minister, and that at least five of them functioned in a regular. In the other six Provinces, the Ministers belonged to the minority, but they advanced swiftly in their nation-building programs; the congress felt it would be lost all if they persisted in their useless policy of denial. Consequently, he accepted positions in 1937; In doing so, he made serious mistakes by excluding members of the Muslim League from the effective participation of the Cabinet. They only admitted Muslims who were congressmen in The gabinet. This was the correct policy for a country with citizen franchises and no community representation; but, by accepting communal electorate and communal franchises as well as other separatist paraphernalia, it became untenable to keep the members of the Muslim League, since they represented the Muslim mass of each Province, in which they were a minority. The Muslim nationalists who became Ministers did not represent them in the sense that members of the League did. Muslim, and by not taking members of it to the Cabinet, Congress repudiated openly its own action by recognizing itself as a communal system by statute. For him On the other hand, Muslims were reluctant to be under the control of Congress; your interest he never needed protection. The Governors were always ready and willing to offer the most sympathetic support, but rejection by members of the Muslim League as Ministers he gave

Mr. Jinnah a tactical advantage which he used to the full; and in 1939, when Congress resigned in a fit of anger, it passed into the hands of the League Muslim and British Imperialism. Under Section 93 of the Government of the India in 1935, the Governors took control of the Governments of the Provinces of the Congress and Ministers of the Muslim League retained power and authority in the Remaining provinces. The Governors went ahead in the administration with a definite inclination towards Muslims as an Imperial Policy of the British; he communal system reigned throughout the country through Muslim Ministries for a side and pro-Muslim Governors on the other. The Hindu-Muslim unity of Gandhiji became a dream, if it ever was anything else; but he never it mattered. His ambition was to become the leader of Hindus and Muslims alike, and at the resign from the Ministries, Congress again sacrificed democracy and nationalism. Religious, political, economic and social rights were sacrificed fundamentals of the Hindus on the altar of the Mahatma's obstinacy.

(i) **League takes advantage of war**—Motivated by the aforementioned situation, the Muslim Government in five Provinces and pro-Muslim Governors in the other six, Mr. Jinnah sped on. Congress opposed the war of a and a thousand ways. Mr. Jinnah and the League had a very clear policy. They remained neutral and did not give any problem to the Government; however, the following year, during the Lahore session of the Muslim League, they passed a resolution for partition of India as a condition for their cooperation in the war. A few months from the Lahore resolution, Lord Linlithgow gave full support to Muslims in their policy separation through a statement of Government Policy that assured them that no would make any changes to the political constitution of India without everyone's consent the elements of the national life of the country. The Muslim League and Mr. Jinnah were vetoed on the political progress of this country through the agreement given by the Viceroy of India. From that day on, the disintegration process advanced with accumulated force. The League did not prohibit Muslims from enlisting in the Navy, in the Navy or Air Force, and they did it on a grand scale. In fact, the Muslims of the Punjab suffered their percentage in the Indian Navy, completely reduced. So with a vision prepared for eventualities in a future Muslim state, as it is in Kashmir today nowadays, of course the Muslim League never gave the government difficulties during the six years of the World War (referring to the speech given by the late Sir Sikandar Hyat Khan in Cairo before the armed forces during the last World War). All they wanted was for no change to be made to the Constitution of India without their full consent, and that this would only be obtained if Pakistan was granted. Lord Linlithgow implicitly gave this assurance in August 1940.

(j) **Cripp's partition proposal accepted** — Congress did not know if support the war, oppose it, or remain neutral. All these attitudes were expressed one after another; sometimes by way of speeches, sometimes by way of resolutions, sometimes by way of through press campaigns and sometimes in other ways. Naturally the Government felt that Congress had no mind of its own, save for verbose condemnations. The war was carried out without consent or hindrance until 1942. The Government could have all the men, all the money, and all the material that his efforts for war required. All loans were made to him. In 1942 came the Cripps Mission, the which he presented to

Congress and the rest of India, a mirage of useless promises, armed that was, with a clear indication of partition of the country in the background. Obviously the Mission It failed, but even when Congress opposed this proposal, it relented early in partition after a rather pretentious resolution reiterating its adherence to democracy and nationalism. At a meeting of the entire Indian Congress Committee held in April 1942 in Allahabad, an overwhelming majority repudiated the principle of partition; the minority consisted of the present Governor General, Mr. C. Rajagopalchari and his half dozen supporters; but Maulana Azad, the so-called Muslim nationalist, was at that time then the President of Congress. It granted a ruling a few months later; the resolution Allahabad had no effect on the previous Labor Committee resolution that granted the remote principle of Pakistan. Congress was stumped. Government British continued to effectively control the entire country through Ministries Muslims and pro-Muslim Governors. The princes were fully identified with the war. The Labor Committee refused to stand aside. The capitalist class supported the Congress by word of mouth and the Government by providing everything it wanted to the best prices. Even the Khadar enthusiasts sold blankets to the government. He Congress could not find a way out of this paralysis; was out of reach and the Government went ahead despite its nominal opposition.

(k) **"Drop India" by Congress and "Divide and Drop" by of the League** — Out of desperation, Gandhiji evolved the "Leave India" policy that Congress had approved. It was supposed to be the biggest rebellion against the foreign dominance. Gandhiji had ordered people to "do it or die." Except that the leaders were quickly arrested and detained; Congressmen practiced some acts of violence for a few weeks, however, in less than three months, the Government strangled the entire movement firmly and discreetly. Movement soon collapse. What remained was a series of pitiful pleas from the Congress and its supporters, who were out of prison, for the release of the arrested leaders without formally withdrawing the movement "Abandon India ", which had already collapsed. Gandhiji even mounted a fast at his faculty liberation, but for two years, until the Germans were defeated, the leaders had to remain imprisoned and our imperial lords triumphed all that weather. Mr. Jinnah openly opposed the "Leave India" movement as hostile to Muslims and launched the counter-slogan "Divide and abandon." That's when Gandhiji's Hindu-Muslim unity arrived.

(l) **Hindi versus Hindustani** — Couldn't more blatantly illustrate the Gandhiji's absurd pro-Muslim policy that in his perverse attitude in questioning the National language of India. By all studies of a scientific language, Hindi possesses the most important demand to be accepted as the national language of this country. To the early in his career in India, Gandhiji gave Hindi a great impetus, but seeing that Muslims disliked him, he became a traitor and emerged as a defender of the which is known as Hindustani. Everyone in India knows that there is no language with that Name; it has no grammar; neither vocabulary; it is merely a dialect; talk, more it is not written. It is a bastard language and a hybridization of Hindi with Urdu, not even the Gandhiji's sophistry could popularize it; However, in his desire to please the Muslims, he insisted that only Hindustani should be the national language of India. By supposed that his loyal supporters supported him blindly, so he began to use the hybrid language. Words like "Badshah Ram" and "Begum Sita" were spoken and written , However, the Mahatma never dared to address Mr. Jinnah as Shri Jinnah or Maulana Azad as Pandit Azad. All his experiments were conducted at the expense of the Hindus. His quest for Hindu-Muslim unity was a one-way street. She was about to prostitute herself the charm and purity of the Hindi language in order to please the Muslims, even congressmen apart from the rest of India, refused to swallow this panacea. He persisted in his support for the Hindustani. However, the Hindu majority proved be stronger and more loyal to his culture and mother tongue and refused to bow to the fiat of the Mahatma. The result was that Gandhiji did not prevail in the Parishad Hindi and that he had to resign from that body; Despite that, his pernicious influence still remains, and Government Congresses in India still hesitate to choose between Hindi or Hindustani as the national language. Common sense should still make it clear to mind more limited than the language spoken by 80 percent of the people would have to be the language official of the country, but his ostentatious support for Muslims made him look almost like a idiot when he continued to side with the Hindustani. Fortunately there are millions and millions of defenders of the Hindi language and Devnagari letters. The UP Government has adopted Hindi as the language of the Province. The Committee appointed by the Government of the India has translated the entire draft of the Constitution into pure Hindi and now prevails for the Congress Party in the legislature to adopt the view of meaning common in favor of the Hindi, or to assert his loyalty to the Mahatma in his evil attempt to impose a foreign language in a great country like India. For purposes practical, Hindustani is the same as Urdu only with another name, but Gandhiji did not have the courage to advocate for the adoption of Urdu against Hindi, therefore, the subterfuge of introducing Urdu disguised as Hindustani. No Hindu nationalist prohibits Urdu, but smuggling it as Hindustani is a fraud and a crime; that is what the Mahatma tried to do. Support a non-existent dialect in the school program and in educational institutions disguised as Hindustani just because It pleased the Muslims was the Mahatma's worst kind of communal system. All this for the Hindu-Muslim unity.

(m) **Vande Mataram is not sung**—Gandhiji's blind love for the Muslims and their incorrigible yearning for Muslim leadership regardless of right or wrong, truth or justice, and with utter disregard for the sentiments of the Hindus as a whole, was the filigree of the benevolence of the Mahatma. It is noteworthy that some Muslims disliked the famous hymn "Vande Mataram" so the Mahatma stopped singing or reciting it as far as possible. For a century this song has been honored as the most inspiring exhortation to the Bengalis to stand up as one man for their nation. In the shaking of anti-partition By 1905, singing in Bengali achieved special distinction and popularity. The Bengalis swore and pledged themselves to the motherland in countless meetings where it was intoned. The British Administrator did not understand the true meaning of the chant that simply said "Save the motherland." That's why forty years ago, for a time, the government banned the singing, which increased its popularity all over the country. It continued to be sung throughout the Congress and other national assemblies; But as soon as a Muslim objected, Gandhiji forgot the national sentiment behind him and he persuaded Congress not to insist on singing it as the national anthem. Now I know has asked us to adopt Rabindranath Tagore's

"Jana Gana Mana" as a replacement for "Vande Mataram". Could anything be more demoralizing or pitiful than this action cheeky against a world famous chant? Simply because an ignorant fanatic disgust. The correct way to proceed would have been to enlighten the ignorant and take away the prejudice, but that is a policy Gandhiji did not have the courage to attempt during his thirty years of unlimited popularity and leadership. His idea of Hindu-Muslim unity it only meant surrendering, capitulating, and granting whatever Muslims wish. No wonder the chimera of unity never came and never would have come to be formed.

(n) **Shiva Bavani is forbidden** — Gandhiji forbade reciting or reading so publishes the Shiva Bavani, a beautiful collection of 52 verses by a Hindu poet who extols the great power of Shivaji and the protection he brought to the Hindu community and their religion. The restriction of that collection says: *"If there were no Shivaji, the whole country would have become to Islam"*. Here I recite the couplet from the book "Shiva Bavani" that ends with the words:

> *Kashiji Ki Kala jati Mathura masjid hoti*
> *Shivaji jo na hote to Sunnat hoti Sabki*

For millions, this was a delight of contemporary history and a beautiful work of literature, but Gandhiji wanted none of it. Hindu-Muslim unity in place.

(o) **Suhrawardy is encouraged** — When the Muslim League refused to join the Provisional Government to which Lord Wavell had invited Pandit Nehru to form, the League began a Council of direct action against any Government formed by Pandit Nehru. On April 15, 1946, a little over two weeks before Pandit Nehru took office, a rampant massacre against

Hindus broke out in Calcutta that lasted three days. The horrors of these days are described in the Calcutta "Statesman" newspaper. In At that time it was considered that a government that allowed such atrocities in against his citizens he had to be expelled; there were suggestions that the Government of Mr. Suhrawardy, but the Socialist Governor refused to take possession of administration under Section 93 of the Government of India Act. However, Gandhiji went to Calcutta and struck up a strange friendship with the perpetrator of these massacres, In fact, he intervened on behalf of Suhrawardy and the Muslim League. During the three days that the massacre took place, the Calcutta police did not interfere to protect life or property, countless atrocities were practiced right under the noses of the guardians of the law, but nothing mattered to Gandhiji. For him, Suhrawardy was the subject of a admiration from which he could not be diverted, and publicly described him as a martyr. It is not surprising that two months later there was the most virulent outbreak of fanaticism Muslim in Noakhali and Tipperah; 30,000 Hindu women were converted to the strength According to a report by Arya Samaj, the total number of Hindus killed or wounded was three hundred thousand, not to mention the tens of millions of rupees in value of properties looted and destroyed. Then Gandhiji carried out, apparently alone, a trip to the Noakhali District. It is well known that Suhrawardy gave protection to wherever she went, and even with her, Gandhiji never ventured into the District Noakhali. All these attacks, loss of life and property occurred when Suhrawardy was the Prime Minister, already such a monster with unfairness, poison communal, it is to whom Gandhiji granted the undeserved title of martyr.

(p) **Attitude towards Hindus and Muslim princes —**
Followers of Gandhiji successfully humiliated the
states of Jaipur, Bhavnagar and Rajkot. Even they
enthusiastically supported a rebellion in Kashmir state
against the Hindu prince. This attitude is in grossly
strange contrast to what Gandhiji did about to affairs
in Muslim states. There was a Muslim League intrigue
in the state of Gwalior, which resulted in four years ago
being forced to Maharaja to abandon the celebrations
of the second millennium of the Vikram calendar;
the agitation was based on the communal system.
The Maharaja is a liberal ruler and impartial with an
alien perspective. In a recent clash between Hindus and
Muslims in Gwalior, just because the Muslims suffered
some casualties, Gandhiji went up with the Maharaja
with a totally undeserved biting attack.

(q) **Gandhiji on a hunger strike —** In 1943, when Gandhiji
was on hunger strike and no one was allowed to
interview him on political matters, only the most near
and dear ones had permission to go and inquire about
their health. Mr. Rajagopalachari he entered Gandhiji's
room and devised a scheme to concede Pakistan;
Gandhiji allowed him to negotiate with Jinnah. Later, in
late 1944, Gandhiji discussed this matter for three weeks
with Mr. Jinnah and offered him virtually what it is now
known as Pakistan. Gandhiji went to Mr. Jinnah's house
every day, complimented, praised, hugged, but Mr.
Jinnah could not be coaxed into agreeing to the Pakistani
demand that would cost dearly. Hindu-Muslim unity
was progressing in a negative direction.

(r) **Desai-Liaquat Agreement —** (i) In 1945 came the
notorious Desai-Liaquat Agreement. He placed
one, almost the last, nail in the coffin of Congress
as a democratic body national. In that agreement,
the late Mr. Bhulabhai Desai, then the leader of the

Congress Party at the Central Legislative Assembly in Delhi, reached an agreement with Mr. Liaquat Ali Khan, Leader of the League in Assembly, to request a conference with the British Government for the solution of the stagnation that was growing in Indian politics since the beginning of the war. It was understood that Mr. Desai took that step without consulting nobody of importance in the congressional circle, since almost all the leaders had been imprisoned since the Resolution "Leave India" in 1942. Mr. Desai offered the Muslims equitable representation with Congress; this was the basis with which approached the Viceroy to arrange the Conference. Upon receiving this request, the then Viceroy Lord Wavell flew to London and brought with him the consent of the Government of Labor to carry out said Conference. His official announcement stunned the country for its falsehood in the face of nationalism and democracy alike, of which Congress he had become a partisan. Indian democracy stabbed in the back and every principle of justice was violated. Members of Congress quickly gave in to this monstrous proposal. However, the proposal had, as later revealed, the blessing from the Mahatma which was in fact done with his prior knowledge and consent.

With the full agreement of the Congress party, 25% of the inhabitants in India they were treated as if they were 50% and 75% were reduced to the 50% level. The Viceroy it also dictated other conditions for holding the Conference. These were:

1. An unreserved commitment on the part of Congress and all political parties to support the war against Japan until obtaining the victory.

2. A coalition that the Government would form, in which Congress and the Muslims would have five representatives. Besides there would be a

representative of the underprivileged classes, of the Sikhs and of other minorities.

3. The "Leave India" movement would be unconditionally withdrawn and The leaders detained as a result would be released.

4. All the measures of the Administrative Reform would be carried out in the Four Corners of the Government of India Act 1935.

5. The Governor General and the Viceroy would retain the same position with the new agreement, just as it had at that time; that's what he would remain as head of the new government.

6. At the end of the war, the question of complete freedom would be decided through the machinery of the Constituent Assembly.

7. If no modification happened, the Viceroy would reconstitute his Government with all the portfolios handled by Indians, as indicated by the point (2) above.

8. The people who just three years ago started the movement "Leave India" and that they exhorted people to "Do or die" to implement the rebellion, he would quietly submit to accept a office under the leadership of a British Viceroy and under the terms and conditions established by it. The fact was that the movement "Leave India" had failed, Congress had no program alternative and events would happen regardless of whether the Congress party was he ready or not. Mr. Jinnah was the sole winner for the collapse of the Congress. He gained a great tactical advantage when the Muslims 50% of the representation in future discussions. The theory of nations and demand for Pakistan received a boost, although the Conference failed to achieve Hindu-Muslim unity.

(s) **Cabinet Mission Plan**—In early 1946, the so-called mission of the Cabinet Cabinet came to India. It consisted of the then Secretary of State for India, now Lord Lawrence, Mr. Alexander, the Minister of War and Sir Stafford Cripps. Mr. Atlee, Prime Minister announced their arrival through a speech in Parliament. He announced in the most eloquent terms the determination of the British Government to transfer power to India if they only agreed to a common plan. The agreement was the axis for mission work, but it was fatal. Congress wanted a united India, but not he was frank in his conviction. It lacked firmness. On the other hand, Mr. Jinnah demanded a India divided, but did it firmly. Faced with these two opposing demands, the mission found it impossible to reach an agreement, and after informal discussions with both, gave know his solution on May 15, 1946. He rejected and gave ten good reasons, but while supporting the unity of India, he introduced Pakistan through the back door. At paragraph 15 of the proposals, the mission disclosed six conditions under which the British Government would be prepared to convene a Constituent Assembly and draw up a Constitution of a Free India. Each of these six proposals was calculated for to prevent unity in India from being maintained, or to prevent complete freedom from even if the Constituent Assembly was an elected body. The party of Congress was so weary of the failure of "Leave India" that after a smokescreen over his unshakable nationalism, he virtually submitted to the Pakistan by accepting the mission proposals that made the dismemberment undeniable of India in a round way. Congress accepted the ruse, but did not agree to form a Government. The point was that Congress was called to form a Government and accept the project unconditionally. Mr. Jinnah denounced the British

Government for treason and started a direct action meeting of the Muslim League. Bengal, the Punjab, Bihar and Mumbai became the scene of massacres, arson, looting and violations on a scale unprecedented in history. The overwhelming number of victims they were Hindu. Congress was horrified but powerless, and failed to provide protection some to the Hindus nowhere. The Governor General, despite his powers to intervene under the 1935 Act in the event of a breach of peace or tranquility in the India or somewhere in it, he just stared and made no use of his obligations. A few hundred thousand people were killed, thousands of women and children were kidnapped and some of them have not yet been traced, thousands and thousands of women were raped, hundreds of tens of millions of rupees in property were looted, burned or destroyed. The Mahatma was, as far as before, from his goal by achieve Hindu-Muslim unity.

(t) **Congress Surrenders to Jinnah** — For the following year, the Party of Congress vilely surrendered to Mr. Jinnah at bayonet point and accepted Pakistan. The what happened after that is well known. The thread throughout this narrative is infatuation on the rise that Gandhiji developed for Muslims. He did not utter a single word of sympathy or comfort for the millions of displaced Hindus; I had just an idea of humanity and this was the Muslim. The Hindus simply did not count on him. I I was surprised by all these manifestations of Gandhian sanctity.

(u) **Ambiguous statement on Pakistan** — In one of your articles, while Gandhiji was nominally opposed to Pakistan on the surface, openly declaring that if the Muslims wanted Pakistan at any cost, there was nothing to stop them from get. Only the Mahatma could understand what that statement meant.

It was one prophecy, statement or disapproval of Pakistan's claim?

(v) **Bad advice to the Maharaja of Kashmir** — About Kashmir, Gandhiji stated time and again that Sheikh Adbullah should be entrusted with the position of the State and that the Maharaja of Kashmir had to retreat to Benares for the simple reason that the Muslims they made up the majority of Kashmir's population. Also, this stands out in contrast to his attitude in Haiderabad, where although the majority of the population was Hindu, Gandhiji he never asked the Nizam to retire to Mecca.

(w) **Mountbatten Divides India** — From August 15, 1946 onwards, the Private armies of the Muslim League began to kill, devastate and destroy the Hindus wherever they could place their hands. Lord Wavell, the then Viceroy, He was undoubtedly distressed by what was happening, but did not use his powers under the Act of 1935 of the Government of India to prevent such a holocaust and that Hindu blood would flow from Bengal to Karachi with mild reactions in the Deccan. All the time, from the 2nd September 1946, the so-called National Government, which consisted of two elements fully reconcilable with each other, was in power, but the members of the League Muslim, who were 50% of the Congress, did everything in their power to make the work of a coalition government impossible. Members of the League Muslim did their best to sabotage it; the more disloyal and treacherous returned to the Government of which they were a part, the greater was the infatuation of Gandhiji did with them. Lord Wavell had to resign because he could not reach an agreement. He had some conscience, which prevented him from supporting the partition of India. Declared openly that it was both unnecessary and undesirable. However, with his resignation followed by the appointment of Lord Mountbatten. King Log was succeeded by King Stork. This supreme commander of Southeast Asia was a born military man and had a great reputation for boldness and tenacity. He came to India determined to make or die, and "made", that is, divided India. He was indifferent to human slaughter. Rivers of blood ran before his very eyes. Apparently he thought that with the slaughter of Hindus, many adversaries of his mission would die; the greater the slaughter of enemies, bigger the victory; He relentlessly pursued his goal to its logical conclusion. Long before June 1948, the official date for the handover of power, the total of murders of Hindus had taken effect. The Congress that had boasted of its nationalism and democracy literally secretly accepted Pakistan at the tip of bayonet and abjectly surrendered to Mr. Jinnah. India was divided. A third part of Indian territory became foreign land as of August 15, 1947. In Congressional circles described Lord Mountbatten as the greatest Viceroy and Governor General that India has ever known. It granted ten months before the 30 of June 1948, known as Dominion status, to section India. This is what Gandhiji achieved after thirty years of indisputable dictatorship, and it is what the Congress party called "Freedom." Never in the history of the world had she been a blind eye to such a massacre, or to its result, described as "Freedom" and "Transfer peaceful power ". If what happened in India in 1946, 1947 and 1948 is called peaceful, one wonders what is violent. The bubble of Hindu-Muslim unity had finally burst and a dissociated theocratic and communal state had been established with the consent of Nehru and his horde, and had called her "Freedom won by them at the cost of sacrifice ". Whose sacrifice?

(x) **Gandhiji sacrifices cows**—Gandhiji used to show a vehement desire towards protecting the cow. But, she didn't really push herself in that direction. Conversely, in one of his speeches after praying, he acknowledged his inability to support the claim to stop the slaughter of cows. An excerpt from his speech is quoted in this regard: Rajendra Babu informed me that he has received about fifty thousand postcards, and between 20 and 30 thousand telegrams urging a ban on cow slaughter law. Regarding this I have already spoken to you before. After all, why have they sent me so many letters and telegrams? Not they have served no purpose. No law can be enacted that prohibit the slaughter of cows. How can I impose my will on someone who does not want to give up cow slaughter? India will not It belongs exclusively to the Hindus. Muslims, Parsis and Christians. They all live here. The claim that India has become the land of the Hindus is absolutely wrong. This land belongs to all live here. I know an orthodox Vaishnava Hindu. Used to give your child beef soup.

(y) **Removal of the tricolor flag**—Congress adopted the tricolor flag with the charkha as the national flag in deference to Gandhiji. There were greetings to the flag on many occasions. The flag was unfurled at every meeting of Congress. It waved in every session of the National Congress. He did not complete pheries prabhat to unless the flag was carried when the march began. On the occasion of imaginary or real success of the Congress, they decorated with that flag both public meetings, such as shops and private residences. If any Hindu gave importance to the flag Shivaji, the "Bhagva Zenda" flag , which liberated India from Muslim rule, was considered communal. Gandhiji's tricolor flag never protected any woman Hindu to be raped or to some temple to be desecrated, even so, enthusiastic congressmen the late Bhai Parmanand was once harassed for failing to pay tribute to the flag. College students showed their patriotism by mounting that flag on the building academic. A Bombay Major is believed to have lost his knighthood because his wife raised this flag at the corporation building. That was supposed to be the loyalty of the people of Congress carried their "National Flag." When the Mahatma traveled by Noakhali and Tipper in 1946 after the brutal attacks on the Hindus, the flag it fluttered in its temporary cabin. However, when a Muslim went there and objected in his Faced with the presence of the flag, Gandhiji immediately ordered that it be removed. In a minute all the reverential feelings of millions of congressmen were offended towards with the flag, because that would please an isolated Muslim fanatic, and despite everything, the great Catholic Mahatma never came close to his so-called Hindu-Muslim unity.

❑

Part III

Gandhiji and Independence

71. A good number of people work under the deception that the movement liberation in India began with the advent of Gandhiji in 1914-15 and was consummated on August 15, 1947, the day we are said to have achieved our freedom thanks to the leadership of the *"Father of the nation"*. Never in history have ladinos fostered a fiction so stupendous that the credulous in this country will swallow more than a thousand years. Far from achieving freedom under his leadership, Gandhiji left India torn and bleeding from more than a thousand wounds. There has always been a movement in India liberation that has never been suppressed. When the Mahratha Empire was finally dominated in 1818, the British thought that the liberating forces were hidden in some part of India, but in reality they challenged the supremacy of the British so much that North India is concerned with the birth of Sikh power. And, when in 1848, the Sikhs were defeated in Gujrat, the rebellion of 1857 was actively organized. so suddenly and with such force and it was so wide that the British Imperialists began to tremble and more than once they seriously considered the advisability of leave India. The story of the great effort on the part of the Indians to overthrow the British yoke is vividly described in the pages of *"War of Independence-1857 "* by Veer Savarkar; By the time the British regained control, Congress National Indian had already established itself once more to challenge their dominance; since 1885, the national desire for freedom began to assert itself, first by means of constitutional laws, and later through military

methods. The latter became the armed resistance imposed by the bomb on Khudi Ram Bose in 1906.

72. Gandhiji came to India in 1914-15. About eight years earlier, the revolutionary movement had spread over a large part of the country. The movement liberation had not died. He had risen from its ashes like the Phoenix. After the arrival of Gandhiji and his manias for truth and non-violence, the movement began to fade. However, thanks to Subhash Chandra Bose and the revolutionaries in Maharashtra, Punjab and Bengal, the movement continued to flourish parallel to Gandhiji's rise to leadership after the death of Lokamanya Tilak.

73. Even the constitutional movements led by the moderates in the Congress recorded some progress toward freedom. In 1892, the Government was forced British to extend the then Legislative Councils. This was followed by the Reforms Morley-Minto in 1909, when the first elected representatives of the people ensured the right to participate in the work of Legislatures both in voice and in vote. Twelve years later, after World War I, the Montague Reforms Chelmsford granted partial Provincial Home Rule and increased the number of members elected to give a permanent unofficial majority to both the Center and the Provinces; and in 1935, came the complete Provincial Autonomy and the responsibility substantial Central, which covered every issue, except foreign policy, armed and some measures in finance. Gandhiji had no appreciation for parliamentary bodies. He called them prostitutes and always incited their boycott. The constitutional progress of 1935, by As little as it seemed, it had been achieved. Of course the 1935 Act was seriously deficient. Especially because of the numerous and vexatious guarantees granted to the interests British and the premium placed on the communal system.

74. It was objected based on the veto granted to the Governors and the Governor General. It is even reasonable that if the Act had not been boycotted under the leadership of Gandhiji, India would long ago have achieved the status of

a Dominion that supposedly we enjoy having lost a third of the territory.

75. I had already mentioned the revolutionary party that existed independent of the Congress. Among his supporters were many congressmen. This section never reconciled the yoke of Great Britain. Between 1914-1919, during the First World War, the Congress began to move to the left, and outside terrorist movements ranged from In parallel with the leftist party from within. The Gadar Party operated simultaneously in Europe and America in an effort to overturn the Dominion British in India, with the help of the Axis Powers. The "Comagata Maru" incident is well known, and it is without a doubt clear that the "Emden" incident on the beach Madras was not due to the knowledge of the German Commander that India was burning for discontent. However, from 1920 onwards, Gandhiji dissuaded, rejected the use of theforce, even though he himself, only a few years before, carried out an active campaign of recruiting soldiers for Great Britain. The Rowlatt report thoroughly described the strength of the revolutionaries in India. From 1916 to 1918, one Briton after another along with his Indian henchmen were shot dead by the Nationalists revolutionaries; the British authorities trembled for its existence. It was then when Mr. Montague came to this country as Secretary of State for India and promised introduce responsibility; even if you have only partially succeeded in redirecting the current of revolutionary fervor. The 1919 Act of the Government of the India for the Jallianwalla Bagh Tragedy, in which General Dwyer shot hundreds of Indians during a public meeting for the crime of protesting the Rowlatt Act. Sir Michael O'Dwyer was noted for his cruel unscrupulous retaliation against those who denounced the Rowlatt Act. Twenty years later he paid for it, when Udham Singh shot him to death in London. Madanlal Dhingra, Kanhere, Bhagat Singh, Rajguru Sukhdeo and Chandrashekhar Azad were the living protest of the youth India against the foreign yoke. They unfurled and held aloft the flag of Independence, some of them

long before Gandhiji's name was ever heard and even when he was the accepted leader by the constitutional movement of Congress Indian National.

76 He had already declared that the revolutionary movement that began in Bengal and Maharashtra later reached the Punjab. The youth associated with him they came from the rabble of society. They were educated and cultured men who belonged to the most respectable and high-status families in their private lives. They sacrificed their lives of comfort and tranquility by the altar of the freedom of the mother country. Were the martyrs whose blood became the cement of the Indian Church of Independence. Lokmanya Tilak built on it and the Mahatma took advantage of the momentum accumulated by this move. It is my firm conviction that each stage of constitutional progress between 1909 and 1935 was made possible as a result of the revolutionary forces working on the background. 77 A moderate opinion condemned the revolutionary violence. Gandhiji the publicly denounced day after day on each platform and through the press. However, there is little doubt that despite the overwhelming mass of people being silent, they supported everything heart the vanguard of the armed resistance that worked for national freedom. The revolutionary's theory is that a nation will always try to wage war on its foreign conquerors. He owes no allegiance to the conqueror, and the mere fact of his domain carries the news that he can be expelled at any time. I know set aside the armed resistance judgment about a person subject to the Lord foreigner under the principle of loyalty of the citizen towards his state. The more I condemned the Mahatma the use of force in the battle for the freedom of the country, the more popular it became. This fact was demonstrated at the Karachi session of Congress in March 1931; in defying Gandhiji's opposition, a resolution was passed during the open session, admiring the courage and spirit of sacrifice of Bhagat Singh when he dropped the bomb on the Legislative Assembly in

1929. Gandhiji never forgot this defeat, and when Gogate shot a few months later at Mr. Hotson, the Governor of Bombay, Gandhiji rejected the charge during the All India Congressional Committee meeting and stated that the admiration expressed by the Karachi Congress towards Bhagat Singh was actually Gogate's action shooting at Hotson. Subhash Chandra Bose challenged this astonishing statement during the meeting of the same. He immediately disagreed with Gandhiji. To summarize, the participation of the revolutionary youth in the struggle for Indian liberation is not by no means despicable, and those who say that Gandhiji secured freedom, not only they are ungrateful but try to write false history. The true story by the freedom of India from 1895 will not be written while the affairs of the country are under the position of the Gandhiano Group. The memorable participation of the youth will be hidden. Not However, it is true that they played a noble and laudable role. 78 It was not just those who approved of the use of force in the battle for freedom to whom Gandhiji opposed. Even those with political perspectives radically different from his own and from those who did not accept his panaceas, Gandhiji made white of his disgust. An outrageous example of his dislike of people he doesn't He agreed is shown in the case of Subhash Chandra Bose. As far as I know, Gandhiji had made no protest against Subhash's deportation for six years, and the election of Bose for the presidential chair of the Haripura Congress was possible only after he repudiated any sympathy for violence. However, in practice, Subhash never followed the rules Gandhiji wanted during his term of office. Yet thus, Subhash was so popular in the country, that even against Gandhiji's stated wish in favor of Dr. Pattabhi, for the second time he was elected President of Congress by a substantial majority, including from Andhra Desha, Dr. Pattabhi province. This upset Gandhiji greatly and expressed his anger in the form of a Mahatma, full of poison concentrated, declaring that Subhash's triumph was his defeat and not Dr. Pattabhi's. Even after this statement, his anger against Subhash Bose was not satisfied. Only for cursing, absent from the Tripura Congress session, staged a rival function in Rajkot with a malicious fast, and until Subhash was overthrown from the Gaddi Congress , Gandhiji's poison was completely sated.

79. This incident about Subhash's reelection to the top of Congress and his eventual expulsion from the presidential office is an indication of the hypocrisy with which the Mahatma controlled and repudiated Congress as and when he wanted. Since 1934, declared repeatedly, with great detachment, that he was not even a member of four annas (16 goes part of a rupee) from the Congress Party and had nothing to do with with the. However, when Subhash was chosen for the second time, Gandhiji lost the control and provided the best evidence that he had interfered with that choice in favor of the Dr. Pattabhi from the beginning; is proof of his fixed and fascinating interest in rivalries and petty squabbles on every echelon of Congress while professing not to be even a member of it.

80. When Congress launched the "Leave India" movement on August 8 1942 under the initiative of Gandhiji, the Government arrested most of its leaders before that they could give it some start; the hitherto non-violent movement was stopped from the start. There was another section in Congress that went underground. They weren't too concerned with following the Gandhian technique and going to prison; to the On the contrary, they wanted to avoid going to jail as much as possible and in the meantime create maximum damage to the Government by cutting communications, committing arson, looting and other acts of violence, not excluding homicide. That section interpreted Gandhiji's statement exhorting people to "do or die" as if given complete freedom to lead carry out all kinds of obstructions and sabotage. In fact, they did everything to paralyze the Government efforts in war to the greatest extent. They set fire to Thanas Police and postal communications were violently interrupted. In northern Bihar and others places,

burned or destroyed about 900 railway stations, and for a time they almost brought the administration to a standstill.

81. These activities were directly opposed to the creed of nonviolence of the Congress and with the satyagrah technique; Gandhiji could neither support nor oppose these activities. If he supported them, his creed of non-violence would have been exposed. Whether opposed them publicly, would have become unpopular with the masses it mattered whether the expulsion of the British from India was achieved with or without violence. Of In fact, the "Abandon India" campaign became more known for the acts of violence in part of Congress than for anything else. Gandhiji's non-violence had died to just weeks after the 'Leave India' campaign began, as the Violence that was committed under that name was not to his liking. The point of view Gandhiano found himself totally absent from the activities of the Congress party and his supporters a few weeks from August 8, 1942. Nowhere did he profess or practiced nonviolence since the supporters of the campaign were, in the words of the Gandhiji himself, prepared to "do or die." It was until Lord Linlithgow, in his correspondence with Gandhiji in 1943, categorically challenged him to acknowledge or reject the violence from supporters of the "Leave India" campaign, which was forced to Gandhiji to condemn the violence. Any penalty, damage, inconvenience or damage done to the war efforts were the result of the violent activities of supporters of the Congress and not from the Mahatma's so-called non-violence. Nonviolence had failed completely; up to a point, the violence seemed to have succeeded; However, Gandhiji had to report her from prison. This is how Gandhiji discouraged the fight for independence while his own strategy had completely collapsed little after August 8, 1942.

82. By this time, Mr. Subhash Chandra Bose, who had mysteriously escaped from India in early January 1941, had already reached Japan after reaching Berlin through Afghanistan. The way Mr. Subhash Chandra Bose escaped

from Calcutta in January 1941 and the difficulties and suffering to which he had to undergo in his way to the Indian border to Kabul, and from there to Berlin, Mr. Uttam Chand he vividly describes in his book "When Bose Was Ziauddhin". Courage and tenacity with which Bose faced all hardships, dangers, difficulties until reaching Berlin made it the most exciting and romantic read. By the time the mission arrived Cripps to India in 1942, he had already arrived in Japan and was organizing an invasion. Before After Subhash left Germany, Hitler had awarded him the title of His Excellency, and arriving in Japan found the Japanese ready to assist him against the British in the invasion of the country. Japan had already joined the war on behalf of the axis with the attack on Pearl Harbor in the United States; Germany had declared war on Russia; and the Great Britain and France successively declared war on Italy, Germany, and Japan. In Japan, the Federated States of Malaya, Burma and other parts of the Far East, Subhash was greeted with enthusiasm and immense support from the Indians established there.

83. The Japanese had intensified their war efforts and occupied Burma, the Dutch East Indies, the Federated States of Malaya and the entire of the Far East including the Andaman Islands. In this way, Subhash was allowed Chandra Bose start an Indian Provisional Government in Indian Territory. By 1944 it was equipped to start an invasion of India with the help of the Japanese. Pandit Nehru stated that if Subhash Chandra Bose came to India with the support of the Japanese, would confront. In early 1944, the Japanese together with the Indian National Navy organized by Subhash thundered at the gates of India and had already entered the Manipur and in a part of the Assam Border. The ANI consisted of volunteers from the Indian population of the Far East and of those Indians who had deserted from the Japanese prisons. That the campaign eventually failed was not Subhash's fault; their men fought like Trojans. The difficulties were too great and his army

was not it was sufficiently equipped with modern weaponry. The ANI had no aircraft and its supply line was weak. Many died of hunger and disease since they did not adequate medical treatment was available for them. But the spirit that Subhash spawned in them was wonderful. They affectionately called him "Netaji" Subhash Chandra Bose, and had adopted the slogan "Jai Hind" under his leadership.

84. Gandhiji opposed Subhash Chandra Bose's invasion of India. Nehru he objected because he did not approve of Bose's support for the Japanese invader. But without matter the differences between Bose and the other Indian leaders, there was no doubt that Subhash was more loved than anyone else for his effort to destroy imperialism Briton without help. If Subhash had lived and entered India in 1945 after the defeat of the Japanese, the entire population would have, as one man, been behind him and would have welcomed him more warmly. Yet again Gandhiji was more lucky. Lokmanya Tilak died in 1920 and Gandhiji became the undisputed leader. He Subhash's success would have given Gandhiji a tremendous defeat, but luck his share again and Subhash died outside of India. So it was easy for him Congressional party professing love and admiration for Subhash Chandra Bose and the ANI e even defend some of his officers and men at the Great State Trial in 1946, right here in Red Fort. They even adopted "Jai Hind," the catchphrase Subhash had introduced to the Far East. They traded under the name Subhash and the ANI; the two issues that led them to victory during the 1945-46 elections were their feigned affection for the ANI and its hypocritical homage to Subhash's memory. For other On the other hand, the Congress party had promised that it would oppose Pakistan and resist All coast. With these two guarantees, they treated the ANI with little courtesy and of course who succumbed to Pakistan in breach of their promise.

85. All this time, the Muslim League carried out treacherous activities, disturbed the peace and tranquility of

India by mounting a murderous campaign against the Hindus. Lord Wavell and Lord Mountbatten looked on without concern. Congress does not dared to condemn or stop these immense massacres in pursuit of his policy of appeasing at all costs. Gandhiji suppressed anything that did not fit his pattern of activities public. That is why I am amazed when they claim over and over again that obtaining the freedom is due to Gandhiji. My opinion is that both pandering to the Muslim League it was the way to get freedom. He only created a Frankenstein that ended devouring its creator by swallowing a third of the Indian territory, placing permanently hostile, censorious, unfriendly, and aggressive neighbor in what was once it was their territory. On obtaining Swaraj and freedom, I maintain that the Mahatma's contribution was negligible. But, I am prepared to give it a place like sincere patriot. However, his teachings produced the opposite result and his leadership ridiculed the nation. In my opinion, SC Bose is the ultimate hero and martyr of modern India. He kept alive and promoted the revolutionary mentality of the masses, defending all honorable means, including the use of force when it will be needed for the liberation of India. Gandhiji and his crowd of egotists tried to destroy it. It is therefore absolutely wrong to represent the Mahatma as the architect of Indian Independence.

86. The real cause of the British withdrawal is threefold, and that does not include the Gandhian method. The triple forces mentioned previously are:

(i) The movements of the Indian Revolutionaries from 1857 to 1932, that is, until the death of Chandra Shekhar Azad in Allahabad; later, the movement of a revolutionary character, not that of the Gandhian type in the nationwide rebellion of 1942; and the armed revolt sustained by Subhash Chandra Bose, the result of which a mindset spread revolutionary force in the Indian Military Forces are the true dynamic factors that shattered the very foundation of the Dominion British in India. Gandhiji opposed all these effective efforts for Liberty.

(ii) Credit should also be given to those who, full of spirit patriotic, they fought the British strictly under the constitutional laws in the Assembly meeting room and achieved a remarkable progress in Indian policies. The intention of this section was take the maximum advantage of what we achieved and fight from then on. This section was generally represented by the late Lokmanya Tilak, Messrs. NC Kelkar, CR Das, Vithhalbhai Patel, brother of Honorable Sardar Patel, Pandit Malaviya, Bhai Parmanand, and during the past ten years by prominent Hindu Sabha leaders. However, the Gandhiji himself and his followers ridiculed this school of men by call them job hunters or power seekers, though they resorted to often to the same methods.

(iii) However, there is another important reason why the British left power and it is the coming of the Labor Government and the overthrow of Mr. Churchill, imposed by dire economic conditions and bankruptcy to which the war had reduced Great Britain.

87. As long as the Gandhian method was on the rise, frustration was the only inevitable result. Every spiritually individual or group he opposed everywhere, revolutionary, radical or vigorous; and constantly pushed his charkha, his non-violence and its true. The charkha, after 34 of Gandhiji's best efforts, had only led to the expansion of the machined textile industry by more than 200 percent. With Regarding the truth, the least I can say is that the veracity of the Congressman average is undoubtedly of a higher order than the man in the street and very much often it is actually a lie masked with a thin appearance of sincerity feigned.

❏

Part IV

Frustration of an Ideal

88. Truly speaking, the idea of Hindu-Muslim unity that Gandhiji had filed when he entered Indian politics came to an end from the moment he Pakistan was established because the Muslim League was opposed to seeing India as one nation; with great obstinacy they declared again and again that they were not Indians. Unit Hindu-Muslim that Gandhiji presented many times was not of this type. What he wanted it was for both of them to take part in the struggle for independence as comrades. That was his idea of Hindu-Muslim unity. The Hindus followed Gandhiji's advice, but the Hindus Muslims, each time ignored him and unleashed a behavior to insult the Hindus, until at last, culminating in vivisection and division of the country.

89. The relationship between Gandhiji and Mr. Jinnah is also noteworthy. When Mr. Jinnah, who was once an ardent nationalist, became a member of category of the communal system, from 1920 presented the fact clear and evident that his intention was to see the interests of the Muslim community and that it would not trust Congress or its leaders at all; that Muslims don't they would support the fight for freedom together with Congress. Furthermore, Mr. Jinnah demanded Pakistan openly. He has preached these doctrines quite openly. Has not deceived no one as far as principles are concerned. This was the behavior of a public Enemy. He could speak without caring for his language to divide this country with ease.

90. Gandhiji saw and visited Mr. Jinnah many times. Every time I begged him he referred to him as "brother Jinnah." He even offered him the position of Prime Minister of all of India, but on no occasion did it show any inclination even to cooperate.

91. Gandhiji's inner voice, his spiritual power, and his doctrine of non-violence of which he boasted so much, fell to the iron will of Mr. Jinnah and proved not have any power.

92. Knowing that with her spiritual powers she could not influence Mr. Jinnah, Gandhji had to change his policy or admit defeat and give others a chance with different political views to deal with him and the Muslim League. Without However, Gandhiji was not honest enough to do so. Could not forget neither from his selfishness nor from himself, even for the national interest. So there was no place for practical politics while blunders as great as the Himalayas were being committed.

93. Steadily, for about a year, after the horrible massacre in Noakhali, our nation bathed in a pool full of blood. Muslims gave free rein horrible and gruesome human massacres followed by reactions from Hindus in some parts. Attacks by Hindus against Muslims in eastern Punjab, Bihar or Delhi they were simply acts of reaction. Not that Gandhiji didn't know that the main cause For these reactions were the attacks of the Muslims towards the Hindus in the Provinces with a Muslim majority. Still, Gandhiji strongly condemned only the actions on the part of the Hindus, and the congressional government even went as far as threatening to bomb the Hindus in Bihar to curb their discontent and reactions against Muslims which were mainly due to riots and atrocities of these in Noakhali and other places. Gandhiji often advocated during his prayers that Hindus in India should treat Muslims with respect and generosity, even if Hindus and Sikhs were slaughtered in Pakistan; and even if Mr. Suhrawardy was the leader of the goondas (thugs), he should be allowed to roam

freely and safely around Delhi. This will be evidenced from excerpts given above Gandhiji's post-prayer discourses:

(a) "We should reflect with a cool mind when we are rolled. Hindus should never be angry with Muslims even if they are mentalized to get rid of their existence. If they put us all facing the sword, we should bravely accept death; maybe, even if they rule the world, we inhabit it. At least not we will fear death. We are destined to be born and to die; so why what do we saddened about it? If we all die with one smile on our lips, we will enter a new life. We will give origin to a new Hindustan ". (April 6, 1947)

(b) "The few Rawalpindi knights who called me today were strong, brave and engrossed in business. I advised them to stay calm down. After all, God is great. There is no place where God does not exist, mediate with him and take his name; everything will be fine. They asked me what would become of those who were still in Pakistan. I asked them why they came here (to Delhi). Why didn't they die there? I still hold the belief that one should remain in the place that has been given, even if it is mistreated and even murdered. Let us die if people kill us, but Let's do it bravely with the name of God on our lips. Even if our men are silent, why should we be angry with someone, they should realize that even if they are killed, they have had a good and proper ending. May heaven make us like this. May God lead us through Same way. This is what we should pray for from the heart. Them I advise (and issue) as I did with the residents of Rawalpindi, by tell them they should go there and meet the Sikh and Hindu refugees to politely tell them to return to their places in Pakistan without help of the Police or the Army ". (September 23, 1947)

(c) "None of those who have died in the Punjab are coming back. To the In the end we will also have to go there. It is true that they were murdered, but then others die of cholera or due to other causes. One who born must die. If those murdered died bravely, they have not lost nothing, but gained something. But what to do with those who have killed people? it's a great question. One can admit that to err is human. A human being is a bunch of mistakes. In Punjab, our protection is owes them (British troops). But is this protection? I still want if a handful of people must protect themselves. They should not fear him to the death. In the end, the murderers will be none other than our brothers Muslims. Will our brothers cease to be after changing their religion? And don't we act like them? What we leave undone with women in Bihar".

94. Gandhiji should have taken into consideration that the desire for retaliation arising in the Hindu mind was simply a natural reaction. They massacred thousands of Hindus in Muslim Provinces just because they are guilty of being Hindus, and our Government was unable to provide help or protection to these unfortunate people. Could it be somehow unnatural that the waves of sadness and pain of the Hindus in Will those Provinces resonate in the minds and hearts of Hindus in others? It was not for nothing illogical, since these reactions were only signs of human warmth. With the sole objective to compensate the pains and calamities of their neighbors and brothers in those provinces and provide protection, is that they resorted to retaliation against Muslims, because the Hindus believed that this was the only way they would stop their atrocities. When the people (Hindus) noticed and realized that the Government of the Indian Union was unable to provide protection to his brothers residing in Pakistan, he thought of take the law into your own hands. The revenge actions taken by the Hindus in

Bihar were the inevitable result of disgust at the gruesome atrocities in other provinces. Sometimes that feeling is as spiritual and natural as kindness.

95. This great revolution has been successful just because of the idea of this kind of feeling of intense discontent against the misdeeds of the rulers. It would have been impossible to put an end to the rule of the Society of the wicked, if not for such feelings of discontent, retaliation, and revenge that arose against the evil dictators. The ancient history events described in Ramayana and Mahabharat, o the more recent wars of England and the United States against Germany and Japan indicate the same kind of action and reaction. It can be good or bad, but that's the way nature is human.

96. Seen from the point of view of Indian politics, I have previously shown this in my narrative, how Gandhiji vigorously opposed various efforts to win the freedom of the country. There was no consistency in his own political tactics and in particular his behavior when the last war was still unthinkable.

97. He first divulged the principle that India should not help in the war between England and Germany. "WAR MEANS VIOLENCE AND HOW COULD IT I HELP "was the saying. However, wealthy peers and followers of Gandhiji greatly increased their wealth by receiving government contracts for the supply of materials for war. It is unnecessary to mention names, since everyone knows wealthy personalities like Birla, Dalmia, Walchand Hirachand, Nanjibhai Kalidas, etc. Gandhiji and his Congress were greatly assisted by each of they. However, Gandhiji never refused to accept the money these rich people gave him. they offered, even if it came from this war drenched in blood. Nor did it prevent this wealthy people to fulfill their contracts with the government to supply material for the war. Not only that, but Gandhiji gave his consent for the contracts with the Khadi Bhandar Congress to supply blankets to the navy.

98. Gandhiji's release from prison in 1944 was followed by the release of other leaders, however, the government had to secure the help of the leaders of the Congress in the war against Japan. Gandhiji not only did not object to this, but in truly supported the Government's proposal.

99. In Gandhiji's politics, there was no room for consistency of ideas and reasons. The truth was only what Gandhiji could define. His policy was based on old superstitious beliefs such as the power of the soul, the inner voice, fasting, prayer and purity of mind.

100. Gandhiji once said:

Freedom achieved through non-violence mil Years later, it is preferred to the freedom gained Today through violence.

That he acted as he said, or that his actions and words were diametrically opposed to each other can be inferred to some extent by the example cited above.

101. It is worth mentioning a recent example of the inconsistency of its doctrine of non-violence. The Kashmir problem followed closely that of Pakistan. Pakistan began a terrible invasion to conquer and swallow Kashmir. The Maharaja of Kashmir requested help from the Government of Nehru, this agreed to do so on the condition that Sheikh Abdullah will be appointed Chief Administrator. In every matter of importance, the President Nehru consulted Gandhiji. There was every chance there was partiality, with Kashmir being the birthplace of President Nehru. And, not to give Because of this bias, President Nehru consulted Gandhiji on whether to send aid military to Kashmir, and it was only with his consent that he sent troops for the protection and defense of Kashmir. Pandit Nehru himself said this in one of his speeches.

102. Our political leaders knew from the beginning that Pakistan supported the invasion of the raiders in Kashmir. From that it was evident that sending aid to Kashmir it meant waging war directly against Pakistan. Gandhiji himself was opposed to the armed warfare, and told the whole world over

and over again. However, he gave his consent to President Nehru to send the army to Kashmir. The only conclusion that can be obtained from what happens in Kashmir is that, today, after achieving freedom for departed India, and with the blessings of Gandhiji, our Government resorted to the war where machinery is used to kill humans.

103. If Gandhiji's confidence in the doctrine of nonviolence was so firm, he must have made the proposal to send Satyagrahis instead of the armed troops and try the experiment. They should have been ordered to send "Takalis" instead of rifles and " Spinning machines " (ie charkhas) instead of guns. It was a worthwhile opportunity I pray for Gandhiji to show the power of his Satyagraha by following his precept as a experiment at the beginning of our freedom.

104. But, Gandhiji did nothing of the kind. He started a new war for his own will, during the beginning of Free India's existence. What does it mean this incongruity? Why did Gandhiji himself trample on the doctrine of nonviolence that so much had he defended? In my opinion, the reason is quite obvious; and this war is He was fighting for Sheikh Abdullah. The administrative power of Kashmir passed to the Muslims, and it is for this reason and only this that Gandhiji consented to the destruction of the invaders through the Armed Forces. Gandhiji read horrible news about the war in Kashmir while fasting to death solely because some Muslims they could not live safely in Delhi. However, he was not intrepid enough to fasting in front of the invaders in Kashmir, nor did he have the courage to practice Satyagraha in against them. All his fasts were to force Hindus.

105 I think it is unfortunate that in the present twentieth century such a hypocritical as the leader of all Indian politics. The mind of this Mahatma was not seen affected by attacks against Hindus in Haiderabad State; and the mahatma he never asked the Nizam of Haiderabad to abdicate the throne. If Indian policy proceeded thus under the direction

and dominion of Gandhiji, including the preservation of the
Freedom obtained today, even in a sectioned India, would
have been impossible. These Thoughts popped into my mind
over and over again and it was filled with them. As they had
After the aforementioned incidents, Gandhiji announced his
fast for the Hindu unity. Muslim on January 13, 1948; then
I lost almost all control of my emotions.

106 For the past four years I have been working with the
editor of a newspaper, and even before this period, I devoted
most of my time to the service of the public. Therefore, as such,
he had a habit of being in touch with all the developments
of the Indian politics. 107 He was fully aware of the idea of
mutual relationships between the three political bodies, that
is, the Muslim League, Congress, and the Hindu Mahasabha.
The Muslim League always referred to Congress as a Hindu
organization, but the Its leaders were ashamed to be called a
Hindu body. Congressmen they felt abused when they were
called "Communal". 108 Actually speaking, if an institution
was going to look out for the interests of a community in
particular without hindering the growth of the national spirit,
why would anyone Would you use the word "communal" in
the sense of an abuse of that institution? Would be adequate
designate an institution that looks out for the interests of any
particular community by destroy the essence of the national
spirit as a selfish organism with "mentality communal".
But, Congress had no such discretion. Congress entitled both
the League Muslim as the Hindu Mahasabha using the word
"Communal" as an expression of abuse. However, what
should be pointed out is that while Congress has yielded to
each demand of the Muslim League, has not paid due attention
even to the politics nationalist of the Hindu Mahasabha and
has deployed distortion propaganda against it and its leaders.

109. When Congress recognized the Muslim League as
a representative of the Muslim community, from a logical
point of view would not have been out of place recognize

the Hindu Mahasabha as representative of the Hindus, or at least the Congress he should have declared that he would see to the interests of the Hindus. However, Congress never did. As a result of all this, despite the existence of such a powerful organism as is the Muslim League that sees for the interests of its own, some Muslims who were still members of Congress, they also looked out for their interests; while not there was no one to look after those of the Hindus. However, the Congress that mocked the Hindu Mahasabha by calling it "Communal" took part in the leaders conference summoned by His Excellency Lord Wavell in Simla, and accepted the principle of representing 50 percent of Hindus. Not only that, but in the case of Gandhiji, the leaders of Congress were prepared to be recognized as representatives of the Caste of Hindus. This position taken by Congress was the most gruesome and communal as the result of the policy they had adopted to appease the Muslims.

110. Was India's ideal of freedom and independence, torn apart by the vivisection, before Congress, after the founding of what our great leaders national, intelligent, and sacrificially working assiduously to uphold the ideal of freedom of the entire nation, who even sacrificed their lives for their ideal of achieving complete democracy, and attempted mutual cooperation between larger communities and minors of this vast country, and in the struggle for freedom, of which parts of the Punjab, Bengal, Sindh, and the NWF Province that now form Pakistan, were nowhere measure less important than any other part in India? So too, could these patriots, with their ideal of freedom from all Bharatkhand, who were, albeit outside the Congress, in the foreground of the revolutionaries who, whether they went with joy to the scaffold or spend their days outside their motherland as exiles, or rot in dark cells of the Andamans dream of freedom as envisioned in the one granted to the country by means of vivisection? Is it correct that the reward for their sacrifices incomparable has been the

establishment of a state founded by religious fanatics of blind faith in one part of the country?

111. However, Congress, under the leadership of Gandhiji, began its surrender to the Muslims, from the time when the 14 demands of Mr. Jinnah until the establishment of Pakistan. It is not a deplorable sight for people to see Congress celebrate the occasion of the establishment of a Government Domain in the rest of the country torn apart and divided by Pakistan to the east and west and with the sharp thorn of Haiderabad to the center. Seeing this collapse of Congress under the rule of Gandhiji, reminds me of the well-known verse of Raja Bhartrihari in the sense:

(The Ganges has fallen from the heavens on Shiva's head, from there to the Himalayas, from there to the Earth, and from there to the sea. In this way, he went down and down and reached a very low step. I know says that truly indiscriminate people deteriorate to the low position of a hundred ways.)

❑

Part V

Climax of Antinational Appearance

112. The day I decided to remove Gandhiji from the political scene, it was clear to me that personally I would lose everything that could be mine. I'm not a wealthy person but he did hold a position of honor and respect among those known as a society of middle class. I have been in the public life of my Province, and the service that I have been able of toasting, until now it has given me a place of honor and respect among my people. The ideas of culture and civilization are not strange to me. I have had before me some programs of constructive work to do them in my future life and I feel like I have had the strength enough to undertake and carry them out successfully. I have stayed healthy and I do not suffer of any bodily illness nor am I addicted to any vice. Even though I'm not a man very enlightened, I have great respect and admiration for those who are.

113. Beginning in the year 1929-30, when Congress launched its first campaign of Civil Disobedience Movement, I entered the life of a public worker. I was just a student back then. Conferences related to this movement and the reports published in the newspapers greatly impressed me, I decided to join the movement and take a career as a public worker. Just after, when this movement was on top of issues related to Muslims, assumed a grave appearance, and a movement to bring about the unification of the Hindus was led intensively by Hindu Sabha leaders such as Dr. Moonje, Bhai Parmanandji, Pandit Madan Mohan Malaviya, as well as some leaders of the Arya Samaj and the workers of the Rashtriya Sawayam Sevak

Sangh. All organisms politicians ardently discussed the question of the Community Prize; is also worthy of It should be mentioned here that in the Hindu Mahasabha Session that took place in the year of In 1935, it was decided to run against Congress for elections to the legislatures, since that his attitude was unjustly in favor of Muslims and detrimental to the Hindus. The Hindu Mahasabha decided this contest against the Congress under the auspices of the late Pandit Madan Mohan Malviya, who was also a veteran leader of Congress.

114. In turn, around 1932, the late Dr. Hedgewar of Nagpur founded the Rashtriya Swayam Sevak Sangh in Maharashtra. His prayer impressed me with great way and I joined the Sangha as a volunteer. I'm one of those volunteers from Maharashtra who joined the Sangha in its initial stage. For some years too I worked on the intellectual side in the Province of Maharashtra. Having worked for the spiritual elevation of the Hindus, I felt it necessary to take part in the political activities of the country for the protection of the rights of Hindus. That is why I left the Sangha and joined to the Hindu Mahasabha.

115. In 1938, I led the first group of volunteers who marched in the territory of the State of Haiderabad when the movement of peaceful resistance of the Hindu Mahasabha, with a demand for responsible government in the state. I was arrested and sentenced to one year in prison. I have a personal experience with uncivilized, rather, with the barbarian rule of Haiderabad, and I have suffered the punishment dozens of strokes for the injury of singing the "Vande Mataram" at the hour of sentence.

116. In 1943, the Government of Bihar issued a proclamation that prohibited hold the Hindu Mahasabha Session in Bhagalpur. The Hindu Mahasabha resolved challenge this prohibition by considering that the government's action was unfair and illegal. The The session was held despite all the precautions taken by the Government to prevent it. I took a leadership role in preparing for the session by keeping hidden for about a month. During this period, while reading the

newspapers, I came across articles that appreciated my work, I also heard people express their approval for my part in the public life. By nature I am not a person with a violent temperament. Badge, the whistleblower, on page 225 of his testimony he stated that I pulled out a knife to stab Mr. Bhopatkar. That statement is totally false. Mr. Bhopatkar is currently directing the lawyers who defend the accused. Of having committed such assault as described by the whistleblower, would you have offered to assist us in our defense? If the incident you allege were true, the least you would have thought would be accept the help of Mr. Bhopatkar.

117. Those who know me personally take me for a person of reserved temperament. But when high-ranking leaders in Congress, with the consent of Gandhiji, they divided and tore the country, which we consider a deity cult, my mind was filled with thoughts of horrible anger.

I want to make it clear that I am not an enemy of Congress. I've always seen that organism as the main institution that has worked for the spiritual elevation of the country. I had and have my differences with their leaders. This will be clearly seen in my letter addressed to Veer Savarkar on February 28, 1938 (RXD / 30), which is written with my letter and signed by me and I acknowledge its content.

118. There was no enmity between Gandhiji and me for personal reasons. For those who speak of Gandhiji's honest motive in supporting Pakistan, I only have to say that I had but the pure interest of our nation in my heart as I took the step extreme against the person of Gandhiji, who was the person most responsible for the terrible event that culminated in the creation of Pakistan. I could foresee the outcome of my action against Gandhiji's life, and I realized that the moment the people knew about it, despite the circumstances, it would change the way they see me. Me status and honor in society and the sympathy people felt for me would be crushed completely. I fully realized that I would be seen as the most despicable being in the society.

119. He had a clear idea about the fiery attacks that would be launched against me in the press. But, I never thought that the fire the press threw at me could intimidate. If the Indian Press had impartially criticized the policy Gandhiji's anti-national company, and if it had prompted people who considered interest of the nation was far greater than the whim of an individual no matter how large outside, Gandhiji and his followers would never have dared to grant Pakistan to the Muslims as easily as they did. The Press showed so much weakness and submission before the High Command of Congress that allowed the mistakes of leaders to bypass and inadvertent, and made vivisection easy with their politics. The fear of that Press, weak and servile as he was, I couldn't shake my resolve.

120. In some barracks it is declared that the people had not had their independence unless Pakistan was granted. However, I took it as a absolutely wrong and false opinion. To me it is merely an excuse to justify the action the leaders took. The leaders of the Gandhian creed often claim that they conquered "Swarajya" with their fight. Had I done so, it would have been ridiculous to say that the British who relented, were in a position to establish the status of Pakistan before the granting of independence could take place. In my opinion, there could only be one reason for Gandhiji and his followers to give their consent for the creation of Pakistan, and it is that these people were used to setting up a show of hesitation and resistance at the beginning and at the end to surrender to the demands of Muslims.

121 Pakistan was granted on August 15, 1947, and how? Was granted Pakistan fooling people and without any regard for feelings or opinions of the people of Punjab, Bengal, NWF Province, Sindh, etc. It was divided into Bharat indivisible in two, and in one of its parts a theocratic state was established. The Muslims obtained the fruit of their anti-national movements and actions in the form from Pakistan. Gandhian creed leaders ridiculed Pakistan's opponents branding them traitors and communal minded, while they themselves helped

the establishment of a Muslim state in India by giving in to the demands of Mr. Jinnah. This event disturbed my peace of mind. However, if even after foundation of Pakistan, this Gandhian government would have done something to protect the interests of the Hindus in Pakistan, it would have been possible for me to control my mind, which had shaken because of this terrible disappointment of the people. However, after delivering Tens of millions of Hindus at the mercy of Muslims in Pakistan, Gandhiji and his supporters advised them not to abandon it, but to stay there. Consequently, Hindus were caught at the hands of the Muslim authorities, unprepared and in such circumstances, one calamity after another happened. When I bring to mind all these events, my body simply feels the horror of a burning fire, even now.

122. Each new day brought with it the news about thousands of Hindus who were massacred, Sikhs numbering 15,000 who had been shot, hundreds of women stripped of their clothes, stripped naked and carried in procession to be sold in the market as cattle. Thousands upon thousands of Hindus had to run for their lives and lost everything that was theirs. A great march of refugees it stretched for more than 40 miles, it moved towards the Indian Union. How did you counter the Government of the Union this terrible event? Ah, throwing bread at the refugees from the air!

123. These atrocities and bloodbaths would have been stopped to some extent if the Indian Government had presented protests against the treatment imposed on minorities in Pakistan, or even, if they had coldly threatened to treat the same train Muslims in India as a retaliatory measure. But, the Government, that was under Gandhiji's thumb, he resorted to quite different means. If it was given voice in the press to the complaints of minorities in Pakistan, they were called attempts to spread disaffection among communities and offenses; the Government of Congress in various Provinces began to demand, one after another, payments under the Emergency Powers Act

from the press. Only I received notes suing for values up to Rs. 16,000 /-, and Only in the Province of Bombay, about 900 cases occurred, as stated in this Cut to the Home Member, Mr. Morarjibhai. Nothing was done to remedy the complaints of the Press even though its delegations serve the Ministers. That was how there was a total disappointment in my attempt to put pressure on the government through peaceful means of the Congress guided by the Gandhian creed.

124. When all these events took place in Pakistan, Gandhiji did not protested or censured with a single word the Government of Pakistan or the Muslims involved. The atrocities that Muslims resorted to in Pakistan to uproot Hindu culture and society are entirely due to the teachings and Gandhiji's behavior. If the policy had been handled in a practical way India, the terrible human carnage would never have occurred, something unprecedented in the history.

125. The most remarkable and important thing is that Gandhiji never cared about the opinion of the people when it came to Muslims. His theme of non-violence was drenched with human blood, making it impossible for people to consider an idea in favor of Pakistan. As long as there is a theocratic state and government alongside the Indian Union, the peace and tranquility of it will always be in danger. Despite all these facts, Gandhiji assumed a propaganda task, which even the most loyal of the League's supporters Muslim surely would not have been able to do, to stop the spread of the unfavorable opinion in people's minds about Pakistan.

126. It was around this time that he resorted to his last hunger strike. Every condition given by him to stop the fast was in favor of the Muslims and against the Hindus.

127. One of the seven conditions Gandhiji imposed to interrupt his strike famine related to refugee-occupied mosques in Delhi. Is condition was in the sense that all the mosques in Delhi that occupied the Refugees were to be vacated or evicted and given to Muslims. Gandhiji managed to get the government

and certain leaders to accept this condition by coercing them through their fasting. It happened that that day I was in Delhi and personally saw some of the events that occurred to ensure that this condition was fully met. Those were the days of intense or extreme cold, and the day that Gandhiji broke his fast It was raining. Due to this unusual weather, the pungent environment made even wealthy people will tremble. Refugee families and families who had came to Delhi for shelter were expelled, and in doing so they were provided with nothing for your refuge or abode. One or two families with their children and women with their little ones belongings they brought with them said: "Gandhiji, give us a place to stay", they even came over and went to the Birla House. But, it was possible that the cries of this poor Hindu people came to Gandhiji who lived in the palatial Birla House. I was a witness with my own eyes from this scene that would have softened even the heart of the most hard. However, thoughts deeper than this began to appear in my mind. Was it for fun that the refugees found these mosques better than their own homes from which they were evicted? Was Gandhiji not aware of the reasons and circumstances that led them to occupy the mosques? There was no temple or Gurudwara in the part of the country that became Pakistan. These refugees had seen with their own eyes their temples and Gurudwaras desecrated by misuse simply for the purpose of insulting Sikhs and Hindus. Refugees came to Delhi fleeing and having to leave everything that belonged to them, and there was no place to shelter them in Delhi. What question could be asked if the refugees brought over and over See memories of their homes and homes in Punjab and NWF Province while They sheltered the edges of the streets or under a tree? It was under these circumstances that they resorted to occupying the mosques. They took shelter under the roof of mosques, and in doing so, were they not used for the benefit of humanity? Yes while Gandhiji imposed the condition that refugees be evacuated from mosques that had occupied, would have asked the Government and the people concerned to provide some alternative arrangement for their accommodation before being thrown out, would displayed a human touch on your demand. If while Gandhiji demanded evacuation of refugees from mosques, would also have imposed a condition in the sense that Muslims should cede Pakistani temples to Hindus, or some similar condition, his teaching of nonviolence, his anxiety for Hindu unity-Muslim woman and her belief in the power of the soul would have been taken or understood as impartial, bouncy and non-communal. Gandhiji was insightful enough to know that if to end his hunger strike he had imposed a condition on the Muslims in Pakistan, I would hardly have found any who showed distress if the fast will end in his death. It was for this reason that he intentionally avoided imposing some condition to Muslims. It was clear from his past experience that Mr. Jinnah was not disturbed or influenced at all by his fasting and that the Muslim League He hardly gave any value to Gandhiji's "inner voice".

128. It would not be out of place to state here that the remains (ashes) of Gandhiji were spread to large cities and many rivers in India and abroad, but these were not were able to spread in the Indus Saint which passes through Pakistan despite attempts to Shri Shree Prakash, the Indian High Commissioner in Pakistan.

129. Let us take the case of 55 tens of million rupees. Here i read From the Indian Information dated February 2, 1948 the following excerpts:

1. Excerpts from the Honorable Sardar Vallabhai Patel's speech at the press conference held on January 12, 1948.
2. Excerpt from the speech of the Honorable Sir Shanmukham Chetty.
3. India's spontaneous gesture of goodwill, and
4. An excerpt from the statement of the Honorable Prime Minister.

Gandhiji himself said about these 55 tens of million rupees that it is always difficult to make a government alter its decision.

However, the Government has altered and changed its original decision to withhold payment of 55 tens of million rupees to Pakistan, and the reason for doing it was the hunger strike. (Gandhiji's sermon during prayer meeting held on or about January 21, 1948). The decision of withholding the payment of 55 tens of million rupees to Pakistan was taken by our Government, which claims to be the Government of the people. However, this was reversed People's Government decision to engage in the Gandhiji fast. For me it turned out It was evident that the force of public opinion was nothing but insignificance compared with Gandhiji's trends favorable for Pakistan.

130. The creation of Pakistan is the result of Muslim hostility towards the National movement of India. This same Government imprisoned a number of people who showed their loyalty to Pakistan as columnists of the fifth. However, the same Gandhiji was Pakistan's greatest supporter and defender, and there was no power that he wielded any control in him or his attitude.

131. In such circumstances, the only effective remedy to rid Hindus from the atrocities of the Muslims was, in my opinion, to eliminate Gandhiji from this world.

132. Gandhiji is referred to as the Father of the Nation, an epithet of great veneration. But if so, he has failed in his parental duty to the extent that he has acted a very treacherous way with the nation by consenting to its partition. If Gandhiji truly would have maintained his opposition regarding the creation of Pakistan, the Muslim League would not have had the strength to demand it and the British would not have created it despite his greatest efforts to establish it. The reason for this is not very difficult to understand. The people of this country were impatient and vehement in their opposition to Pakistan. But, Gandhiji played with people and gave parts of the country to Muslims for the creation of Pakistan. I firmly hold that in doing so, Gandhiji failed in the duty that it corresponded to him to carry out as Father of the Nation. He has proven to be the Father

of Pakistan. It was for this reason alone that I, as the obedient son of Mother India, believed my duty to put an end to the life of the so-called Father of the Nation, who had played a role important in causing the vivisection of the country, our mother country.

133. The Haiderabad case also has the same story. It is not necessary refer to the heinous misdeeds perpetrated by the Ministers of Nizam and the Razakars. Laik Ali, the Prime Minister of Haiderabad, had an interview with Gandhiji during the last week of January 1948. It was evident from the way he viewed these Haiderabad, that Gandhiji would soon begin his experiments in nonviolence in the Status and would treat Kasim Razvi as his adopted son just as he did Suhrawardy. It was not difficult to see that it would be impossible for the Government, for all its power, to take strong measures against the Muslim state like Haiderabad while Gandhiji was there. If the Government had decided to undertake any military or police action against Haiderabad, would have been forced to withdraw it as happened in the case of the payment of the 55 tens of million rupees on behalf of Hindu-Muslim unity, because Gandhiji would have fasted to death and the hands of the Government would have been tied to save his life.

134. The practice of non-violence, according to Gandhiji, is to endure or endure strikes by the aggressor without showing any resistance either by weapons or physical force. As Gandhiji described his nonviolence, he gave the example of a "tiger turning follower of the creed of non-violence after the cows allowed him to kill them and devour them in such quantity that the tiger ended up getting tired of doing it ". It will be remembered that in At his home in Kanpur, Ganesh Shanker Vidyarthi fell victim to a bloody attack in hands of muslims. Gandhiji often cited this submission to the blows of the Muslims as an ideal example of accepting death for the creed of non-violence; i have believed and firmly believe that the type of non-violence described above will lead to nation to ruin and make it easier for Pakistan to enter and occupy what remains of it.

135. In short, I told myself and foresaw that I would be ruined and that the only thing I could hope for from people would be nothing but hatred, and that I would lose all my honor, even more valuable than my life, if I killed Gandhiji. But at the same time, I felt that politics India, in the absence of Gandhiji, would surely be practical, capable of retaliation, and powerful with the armed forces. No doubt my future would be totally ruined, but the nation would be saved from the advances of Pakistan. People could get to call me and qualify me as devoid of any sense or fool, but the nation would be free to follow the course founded on reason, which I consider necessary to cement the nation building. After fully considering the matter, I made a final decision about the matter, but I didn't speak about it with anyone. I steeled myself with both hands and yes I shot Gandhiji on January 30, 1948 on the ground to pray at Birla House.

136. There is hardly anything left for me to say. If devotion to one's nation It means a sin, I admit that I have committed it. If it is meritorious, I humbly claim that merit. I believe completely and in confidence that if there is another court of law beyond founded by mortals, my act will not be construed as unjust. If after the death there would be no place to reach or to go, then there is no more to say. I resorted to action that I did simply for the benefit of humanity. I accept that I shot the person whose policies and actions had brought torment and ruin and destruction to hundreds of thousands of Hindus.

137. Really speaking, my life also came to an end when I shot Gandhiji. Since then I have spent my days in a trance and meditation. What i have seen and observed during this time has given me complete satisfaction.

138. The problem of the State of Haiderabad, which had been delayed and unnecessarily postponed, after Gandhiji's death, the Government has resolved it properly through the use of armed force. The current Government of the Remaining India take the course of practical politics. The Origin Member is said to have stated that the nation

must possess armies fully equipped with weapons modern and combat machinery. While expressing this, he added that such a step it would be given in keeping with the ideals of Gandhiji. You can say it for your satisfaction. Without However, one should not forget that if that were so, there would be no difference between the means to protect the nation from Hitler, Mussolini, Churchill or Roosevelt with the ruse based on Gandhiji's non-violence. Then it would be impossible to say that there was a new message and Gandhiji's special non-violence.

139. I am prepared to admit that Gandhiji underwent suffering for the good of the nation. In effect it produced an awakening in the minds of the people. Neither did nothing for their benefit; But it pains me to say that he wasn't honest enough to recognize the defeat and total failure of the principle of non-violence. I have read the lives of others intelligent and powerful patriots who made sacrifices even greater than those of Gandhiji. I have even personally seen some of them. But whatever it is, I I bow out of respect for the service that Ganhdiji rendered to the nation, and for the same to Gandhiji; And before I shot him, I actually bowed. However, I hold that even this servant of the country had no right to divide the nation, the image of our worship, deceiving people. Still he did. There was no legal machinery by which a offender like that could be punished, and that's why I resorted to shooting Gandhiji, for it was the only thing he could do.

140. If I had not performed this action, of course it would have been better for me. However, the circumstances were beyond my control. So strong was he impulse from my mind, that I felt that this man should not be allowed to have a death natural, so that the world would know that he had to pay with his life for his favoritism unfair, anti-national and dangerous towards a fanatic section of the country. I decided to end this matter and the future massacres of

hundreds of thousands of Hindus who were not to blame. May God forgive him for his selfish nature which proved too disastrous for the beloved children of this Holy Land.

141. I do not feel animosity or enmity against anyone in particular. Neither I think there is someone hostile towards me. I accept that I had no respect for the present Government due to its policy, which unfairly favored Muslims. But At the same time, I clearly see that this policy was due to the presence of Gandhiji. Without However, in the absence of such pressure, the way is now clear for establishment of a secular state in the true sense of the word. I have to say It is with great regret that the honorable Prime Minister Pandit Nehruji forgets that his actions and works sometimes contradict each other when he speaks of a secular state regardless of time or station; because it is significant to emphasize that he himself has taken an important role in yield to the establishment of Pakistan, a theocratic state. He must have realized that he never it will bring prosperity to the Indian Union with a State founded on a fanatical and blind faith. After All things considered, my mind drove me to take action against Gandhiji. No one exercised or could put pressure on me to take this action.

142. The Honorable Court may take any position regarding the impulse that my mind received and the action I took under it, and can dictate the sentencing orders that it deems pertinent. I don't want to say anything about it. I do not want may I be shown some mercy. For my part, I don't want anyone to ask mercy to me.

143. There are several people here with me treated like conspirators. I already said that in the action I committed I had no companions and that I am solely responsible for it. If they were not charged, I would not have presented any defense, as I would be clear by the fact that I would want and order my lawyer not to question anyone of witnesses connected to the incident of January 30, 1948.

144. I have already made it clear that I personally never accepted the idea of a peaceful demonstration, even on January 20, 1948, including for effective propaganda. However, I agreed to join such a rally at Gandhiji's prayer meeting, albeit with great reluctance. But luckily I couldn't be part of it. And when I knew that this could not be done for one reason or another, I was disappointed and despaired. The efforts of Mr. Apte and others to secure volunteers from Bombay, Poona and Gwalior they did not bear fruit. Then I did not see another way, but the end.

145. With these thoughts in mind, as I scrolled through the refugee camp in Delhi, I met a photographer with a camera on his back. I asked to photograph me. It appeared to be a refugee. I accepted and he photographed me. Returning to the Station of the Delhi Railway, I wrote two letters to Apte to give him a vague idea of my state mentally attaching my photographs, as I believed that it was my duty to inform Mr. Nanarao Apte for being one of my close associates in the newspaper business; one of these I sent one letter to his address in Poona, and the other to the Hindu Rashtra Office.146. I would like to add that all the statements made by me regarding this are totally true and correct and that each of them was made with reference to books authorized. I have made use of several publications of Information India, an organ Government of India official to inform the public, The Indian Yearbook, History of the Congress, Gandhiji's Autobiography, Congressional Bulletins issued from time to time when and the archives of Harijan and Young India, and the post-prayer discourses of Gandhiji. I have not made this long statement because I want people to praise me. My only The objective in doing so is to leave no room for any misunderstandings about me, and that there vagueness in their minds about my criteria.

147. May the country, better known as Hindustan, be united again and become one and that people be taught to

get rid of the defeatist mentality that made them submit before the aggressors. This is my last wish and prayer to the Almighty.

148. Now I am done, but before I sit down I must express sincere and respectfully my gratitude to Your Honor for your patience in listening to me, the courtesy showed and the facilities given. Likewise, I thank my legal advisers and attorneys for their help during this great trial. I do not feel animosity towards the officers police connected with this case. I sincerely thank you for the attention and treatment that they gave me. In the same way, I thank the prison authorities for the good treatment that they toasted me

149. It is a fact that in the presence of a crowd that numbered 300 or 400 people I shot Gandhiji in broad daylight. I made no attempt to escape; of In fact, I never had the idea to run away. I didn't try to shoot myself; it was never my intention to do so, Well, it was my burning desire to express my thoughts in a public audience.

150. My confidence about the moral side of my action has not been affected even with the criticisms made against her. I have no doubt that honest historians they will ponder my act and find its value someday in the future.

AKHANDA BHARAT AMAR RAHE
VANDE MATARAM

(Special Judge)   (Nathuram V. Godse)

Delhi, 8.11.1948

❑

The Allegations Before
the Special Judge,
Trial and Appeals to High Court

The statements of the accused, which were recorded from November 8, 1948 up to November 22, 1948, they amount to 260 pages. In turn, the defense presented 119 documents.

Of the other defendants, Madan Lal Pahwa has confessed that he lit the iron of powder cotton in the precinct for prayer meetings on January 20, 1948 while giving Gandhiji's post-prayer speech. His action was just to record his protest against Gandhiji's pro-Muslim policy, which was against national interests, and there was neither a conspiracy nor was he a member of it.

Digamber Badge, having become an informer, his statement was limited to favor the history of the accusing party.

Nathuram Godse has unequivocally stated that it was he who deliberately fired the pistol with the intent to murder and gave his elaborate reasons for doing so done. He denied the conspiracy charge. All the other defendants denied the charge for conspiracy, or claimed not to know about it.

The arguments of the Prosecutor's Office and the Defense began on 1.12.1948 and they continued day after day. Nathuram V. Godse litigated his own case, while Shri PR Das de Patna argued the case on behalf of Veer Savarkar. They cannot be omitted from being mentioned two events in the Courtroom.

At the trial, Nathuram said that two bullets had come out of the gun, while the medical report found three.

Shri CK Daphtary presented that the accused (Nathuram) He put forward this "two-bullet" argument to support the "benefit of the doubt." Nathuram soon he stood up and replied:

> The pistol was automatic. The trigger was pressed only once. If they came out two bullets or three is immaterial, since only one was enough, and that was the I shot. If with this discrepancy the "benefit of the doubt", the same can be granted to the accusing party.

The other was when Shri CK Daphtary, halfway through her argument, referred to the incident of murder as an "immoral" act. Nathuram got up and objected to it.

> At least, as far as this case is concerned, the Prosecutor's Office has no right to discuss the morality of the act, nor the Court, I humbly argue that they have no jurisdiction to decide that matter. It is seen that the concepts morality changes from society to society, from country to country and from century to century. In a particular society it would be considered immoral for women do not wear a veil (brown), while in others it can be perfectly moral. In some countries drinking liquor would not be considered immoral at all. In a certain century, teaching Vedic traditions to non-Brahmins was I would have seen it as highly immoral, but not today. Such is the way that the concepts of morality are changing. No one, therefore, will be able to determine a standard norm for judging morality or immorality for all times, regardless of country or environment.

> If the Prosecutor's Office wants to maintain that killing is absolutely, totally and without no "immoral" exceptions, then it will have to be admitted that current rulers behave in the most immoral way, because in Sometimes they have to resort to shooting people.

> The Prosecutor's Office has neither the legal nor the moral right to bring this question. If government attorneys were paid a little more than they now perceive, they would undoubtedly work as defense attorneys. Could it, therefore, be said for this alone that they have abandoned the morality or the moral side? The Court only has jurisdiction to decide the legality or not of my act, but as far as morality

is concerned, I am convinced that what I did was totally moral and, regarding that conviction, this Court does not has jurisdiction.

The arguments concluded on 12/30/1948. It gave us the impression that in a month I would deliberate the judgment. February 10, 1949 arrived. We arrived at the Tribunal. According to Judge Shri Atmacharan of the Red Fort Special Court handed down the sentences of the defendants a after the other, the suspense in their minds came to an end, and they were able to save the skillfully composure.

Nathuram and Nana Apte were sentenced to "be hung by the neck to death", while Vishnu Karkare, Madan Lal Pahava, myself (Gopal Godse), Shankar Kistaiyya and Dr. Parchure we were sentenced to "banishment for life." Digambar Badge was offered a pardon as he became an informer, while Veer Savarkar was acquitted honorably. There was an uneasy calm after the pronouncement of the judgment, and then everyone we convicts exclaim in unison:

Swatantrya Lakshmi ki Jai, Victory for the Hindu Nation;
Long live undivided India! Vande Mataram.

The day of our sentence seemed to pass soon, due to its novelty and the rapid succession of events that took place. When we get up the next morning, we we realized that we had passed into a whole new world. Our dream is He was constantly disturbed by the shackles. No matter how vile our condition, we expressed happiness in thinking that at least there was no acquaintance who see us in that state.

We were allowed a period of fifteen days to file appeals against the verdict of the Special Court. Our attorneys were busy with the presentation of our appeals. So they visited us two or three days later, but none of we had a trace of sorrow or misery on our faces. Nathuram did not appeal the charge filed under Section 302 of the Penal Code and the sentence that was passed under it. its The appeal was against the other charges that were to be established. After two months, we were removed via Panipat to the Centro Ambala Prison in a truck from the Policeman.

Nathuram and Nana were taken to the cells of the condemned. At the five remaining they sent us to a patio. We could go to the death cells and see Nathuram and Nana often. The sympathetic attitude of the officers in Ambala prison was our greatest satisfaction. Perhaps it was due to two causes.

These authorities watched us all very closely for a few days. Not they found evidence of a criminal tendency in none of us. Second, in the Deep in their hearts they knew why Gandhiji was killed.

We received the books from the printed files of the Case on the Death of the Mahatma Gandhi on April 14, 1949, with only fifteen days remaining for the hearings. On the spot, Nathuram began studying these books and jotting down notes.

The question of whether Nathuram Godse would be allowed to defend himself in person or be it would oblige the acceptance of a defense attorney provided by the Government as its "intercessor", also attracted a judicial adjudication, and this was given on March 24, 1949 and was reported as Nathuram V. Godse vs The Crown. (AIR 1949 Eastern Punjab 321). The Court accepted his petition and allowed Nathuram Godse to appear in person and plead his case. Was brought to Simla.

Nathuram's 40th birthday was May 19, 1949 while he was in Simla. Our younger brother, Dattatraya, who was released from Prison detention Yeravada Central (Pune, Maharashtra) a few months earlier, he went to Simla to attend the Court and hear the process.

On the afternoon of May 19, I was ready to go see Nathuram and congratulate him on his birthday, when a girl came to see him. Incidentally, Dattatraya had seen her in the Court.

The girl asked Dattatraya to take her to Nathuram because she wanted to see him. "But," Dattatraya told him, "only relatives are allowed." She confided to him: "I'll handle it. Just take me to the cell where they are staying".

Then he revealed his identity. She was the daughter of a Superior Court judge who was seated, but not in the bench where the appeals were heard. I had a small basket with fruits and some flowers. Authorities noted Dattatraya's name as the only visitor and allowed the girl to accompany him.

The girl greeted Nathuram and offered him the flowers and fruit. With few words expressed appreciation. From the bottom of the basket he took out a sweater. He wanted to give it to Nathuram. He An officer on duty reviewed it and gave him permission.

"Wear this sweater one day you defend the case. It would make me feel happy." She said. Nathuram thanked him and agreed to put it on.

The late Maulana Azad noted in his book, "India wins freedom", in the page 225, "Some women from respectable families sent (Nathuram) a sweater that they had woven for him ", for which he wanted to show how even the elite classes also they considered Nathuram a hero. It was a fact. It was like a hero cult.

The Bank of the High Court of Eastern Punjab, comprising the Judges Amarnath Bhandari, Achhru Ram and Gopaldas Khosla, began the final audience for our appeals on May 23, 1949. The hearing continued day after day for fifteen days.

Concerning Nathuram's stay in Simla, special mention should be made of the curiosity that aroused among the people, because he himself would take his own case, and that with the sword of Death hanging over his head, since it was public knowledge that he had not appealed against the death sentence handed down by the Special Judge in Red Fort. People wondered how Nathuram achieved that equanimity of mind to defend your case consistently. The audience consisted mainly of the intellectual people who formed the main section of the then Simla population.

Judge Shri Khosla [who was at the Punjab High Court Bench Oriental], in his recent book, "The Assassination of the Mahatma," said this:

> The climax of the appeal we witnessed was the speech given by Nathuram Godse in his defense. He spoke for several hours arguing, in first instance, the facts of the case and then the reason that led him to strip the life of Mahatma Gandhiji.

> The audience moved visibly and audibly. There was a deep silence when he stopped talking. Many women cried and the men they coughed and searched for their handkerchiefs. The silence was accentuated and became more deep with the occasional sound of a soft sob or cough off.

> I have no doubt that if a jury entrusted with the task of deciding Gandhiji's appeal would have constituted the hearing, with a The overwhelming majority would have rendered an "not guilty" verdict.

The Superior Court judgment was delivered on June 22, 1949. Dr. Parchure and Sharkar Kistayya were acquitted. Convictions of everyone else, including sentences of death of Nathuram Godse and Nana Apte, remained.

❏

Events After
the Superior Court Trial,
Up to the Execution of
the Death Sentence

After the appeal hearing ended, Nathuram was brought back to the Central Ambala prison and placed him in the prison cell in mid-June 1949. Nana Apte was already there. They both stayed there until the end.

While Nathuram was in temporary custody in Simla, he received a letter that authorities obligatorily censored and handed him over. It was from **Shri Ramdas Gandhi**, one of the sons of Gandhiji. The letter read:

Khalasi destination, Nagpur, CP
Dated May 17, 1949.

Dear Nathuram Godse,

The writer of this letter is the son of someone to whom it seems that you is proud to have killed.

I am sure, someday you will find that you have only put end to my father's perishable body and nothing else. Because, not only in me case, but in that of millions around the world, my father's spirit still rules in their hearts. This is proven by the tributes that the Nations and people have surrendered to my father around the world.

You know that today everyone in the world is thirsty and sighing for peace. But, you were horrified to find that among the most great military leaders of the present time are said and believed to be not the atomic energy which will bring peace to the world, but the mutual understanding and respect for one another, better understood by the millions of this country with the simple and meaningful words "Satya and Ahimsa".

I hope the mentioned data will help you in dissolving the fog of misunderstanding with which it seems that his mind and vision seem be wrapped, once you free your mind from it. I have no doubt, you You will regret it and realize that what you did is an act that you should not never be repeated, but rejected for all time, whether in the interest of one's religion, or political creed, or whatever else. I know reports that you have recently declared that you are a man of "reason and logic". Therefore I ask you to consider my reflections, and if you do, you will find that it has not served the cause in the least so much for you by doing what you did.

Sincerely,

Sd / -R. Gandhi

PS Let me inform you that on 1.5.1949 I sent a letter to the Governor General of India, giving you my reason why you shouldn't be made to suffer the penalty imposed by the Superior Court and so that investigate the charges that the corresponding authorities raised in your against.

Sd / -R. Gandhi

Nathuram replied:

"OM"

Simla

June 3, 1949.

Dear Brother Shri Ramdas Gandhi,

I received your letter of May 17, 1949 yesterday. As human being no I have words to express my feelings for the wounds that you and his relatives must have received for the tragic end of his revered father, for my work. But at the same time, I declare that there is the other side to be seen. Not I am in a position to write down all my thoughts or even to see it personally. But certainly you he's in a position to see me in jail before my execution.

You say that you have heard that "I am a man of reason and logic." True. But, you will be surprised to notice that I am a man of powerful feelings too, and the "Devotion" to my mother country is the highest of these. You say once my mind is free from misunderstandings, then without a doubt I will regret and realize my error.

Brother I say I'm an open minded man always subject to correction. But what is the way to get rid of my misunderstanding? And if there is, to regret it?

Certainly not the gallows, nor a great show of mercy, and commute my punishment. The only way is to see me and make me realize of it. So far I have not come across anything that makes me regret it.

I have received several letters from some important Christian Missions, and in accordance with their faith and teachings of the "Holy Bible", they have tried give me some message. His posture is quite intelligible. However, the hers is the first I have received which somewhat resembles the well-known or better known teachings of his revered father. In truth this is surprising. I have received many letters full of insults. I don't think they were written by his father's disciples. Either way, I must ask you to come see me, and if it is possible, with some prominent disciples of his father, notably who are not interested in any political power, and make me I know my fatal mistake.

Otherwise, I will always believe that this show of mercy it's nothing but nonsense.

If he really sees me and talks to me, be it sentimental or reasonably, who knows if he will be able to change me and make me regret? Or, if I change him and make him realize my position? The condition for the talk will be that we must adhere to the true only.

I once again express my condolences as a human being for your suffering due to the death of his father by my doing.

Sincerely,
Sd / - Nathuram V. Godse.

N.B. If you prefer, then please send a copy of this to Your Your Excellency, the Governor General of the Dominion of India.

Shri Das Gandhi's other letter reads like this:

Khalasi destination, Nagpur
Dated June 13, 1949

Dear Shri Nathuram Godse,

I received your letter dated June 3, 1949.

Glad to know that you are always willing (literally free) to accept opinions. Similarly, the desire you expressed to speak freely with me and with close associates of my father on the questions whether the ways and means you adopted were helpful or approach to be one day in the future to preserve the integrity of our motherland or our centuries-old Hindu religion, which is, as any other current religion, apart from any type of differences that provokes.

In the same way, without promising to dialogue with you on behalf of the Government of India, as well as on behalf of myself or those who accompany, I am asking Pandit Jawaharlal Nehru to grant us the permission to Shri Vinoba Bhave, Shri Kishorital Mashruwala and me to talk with you about the aforementioned topic, since it is your most sincere so be it.

If fate decrees that the projected talk take place, this will occur only after June 25, 1949, because you should note that I It is possible to travel from Delhi to Nagpur and from there continue to the place where you have retained before June 25.

I think he should not have stipulated the condition "we must speak with attachment to the truth ", because not only do I think it is unnecessary in my case, but also in that of those close to my father.

In the meantime, I would like to suggest that you spend all your free time dispose of introspection and also entrust himself with all his faith to the Almighty. He should pray that "Only he will grant you his most favorable ", because I feel that only this favor will help you to realize your error. And, you will realize that deep down, Gandhiji knew well how protect our motherland and, in particular, the Hindu religion from insults or insults. If you do, I trust that by the end of the projected meeting between you and me, you will be able to recite with us the following verse from the 18th chapter of the Bhagavat Gita, which is a poem perfect in beauty and meaning:

Or, Achyuta, because of your favor my ignorance has disappeared. I have recovered normality. Along with this I have all doubts resolved. I will do what you say.

Sincerely,

Sd / - RM Gandhi

Response sent by Nathuram:

Central Prison,

Ambala,

June 24, 1949.

Dear Shri Ramdas Gandhi,

I received your letter dated June 13 on the 23rd of the same and I wrote down the contents.

I am glad that you have responded to my request. Can come in any time that is convenient for you. You can also see me one day before the execution. I am not impatient for this meeting. I also feel a kind of satisfaction with his intention to meet me. If not see me at all due to other difficulties, I won't feel anything about it because in his heart he showed a willingness to do so. The sincerity of its purpose is reflected in this. It is enough for me.

However, I asked him to try to get this meeting done.

I agree with your statement that I should not have stipulated that "only the truth should be spoken ". Believe me when I wrote it it was not my intention hurt him. There were mainly two ideas in my mind behind that writing. I have met many so-called devotees of the "Truth" creed. Without However, they don't really bother in the least about that creed. I have seen people distort the truth under oath at the bar of the witnesses.

And, another reason is that I may have to say some truths bitter in our conversation. At least according to my belief, It will be true and it will be bitter. Whatever it is. I am so confident from your letter that I shouldn't fear speaking without fear.

I thank you for reminding me of the verse "My ignorance has missing". I have been restored to normal by the

Bhagwat Gita. In my opinion no only these verses in the Gita, but everything is an invaluable poem full of meaning and beauty.

After Arjun said "I will do what you say", directly he translated into practice Lord Krishna's words, "Remember me and fight."

Shri Vinoba Bhave is Maharashtrian by birth. Make one research, if possible, on my general character and behavior prior to incarceration, through him (V. Bhave) or any other. Maybe It is helpful for you to know the background of the subject who committed the cruel act illegal.

Nothing else for now.

Sincerely,
Sd / - NV Godse
June 24, 1949

Apart from the aforementioned correspondence which amply shows the mental balance of Nathuram, his deep conviction and even his open mind to other thoughts. Their words were:

If Gandhiji's disciples convince me that I have done wrong, I will declare my repentance without asking for any reward and go to the gallows. On the other hand, if I convince them of the justification of my act, they they will be honest enough to admit it openly.

Escaping from the gallows doesn't appeal to me. So also in that case I'll come up with liking the platform towards the rope.

That a man of Nathuram's caliber was the cause of the death of a politician important as Gandhiji, who, as everyone knows, had an parallels on Indian political life over a period of nearly thirty-five years until his murder, made it imperative for people to reexamine his background. The next chapter It contains details about him and the other defendants.

That Nathuram stood firm to the end need not, I think, prove himself adducing more evidence than has been cited so far. From the day of the murder of Gandhiji until Nathuram's death by hanging, a period of twenty-one months elapsed and half or six hundred and fifty-five days. During all these days it was observed systematically the daily routine of Nathuram. Even their daily religious rituals.

He did not object to eating or drinking, nor did he suffer from insomnia. On November 11, 1949, our parents sent him a telegram blessing him, to which Nathuram wrote a consoling letter, the summary of which translated says the following:

Amabala, 11.12.1949

My most revered Mother and Father,

I have your photographs here with me, which I will adore until I handed over and joined Brahama.

I do not doubt that you are bound to feel extreme pain and heartbreaking for my loss, because of our worldly relationship in this lifetime. However, I do not write this letter to vent my sorrow or to philosophize with her.

You are students of the Gita and have also learned the Puranas. Lord Krishna recited this Gita to enlighten Arjun; and the Lord himself Krishna, with his Sudarshan wheel, cut off the head of an Aryan king Shishupal, not on the battlefield, but on the ground to sacrifice, the Rajsooya Yadnyabhoomi! Who would say that Lord Krishna committed a sin by do what? Giving gifts or donations to the wicked is not considered an act virtuous, but irreligious. For the sake of a Seeta who is taken by force for a Ravana a huge war must be fought; and for an insult from a Draupadi must wage an epic war in Mahabharata. Right here in our country, in our presence, hundreds and thousands were disrespected of Hindu women who were raped and forcibly taken to be converted to Islam, and the perpetrators of these heinous acts were helped in every possible way. In such circumstances, he could not keep quiet and watch without doing anything, afraid of losing my life or of incurring censorship and public anger. I'm sure the blessings of thousands of young women are with me and support me.

I have placed my life at the feet of my beloved motherland.

My mind is pure and my feelings are absolutely fair. Begging for my life as if begging for mercy by begging for mercy is something I've never liked.

Death did not come to me to ask for my life; I myself have gone to Him to offer it to you.

There are millions of people who will shed their tears at this sacrifice of our lives. They will share your pain.

Akhand Bharat Amar Rahe!
Vande Mataram.

Nathuram continued to read and write regularly until the end. Just the day prior to the execution he finished a lengthy letter written to Shri GT Madkholkar along with others, and also signed the autograph books of some of the visitors who had obtained permission from the authorities.

The current execution process is not something really gruesome in a sentence of death; death comes to the condemned convict without any agony worth mentioning. He great horror for the convict lies in passing one terrible moment after another in absolute loneliness while waiting all the time for the hangman's rope.

In fact, the death sentence is not an imprisonment sentence, but only in a technical sense. Due to the inevitability of the law, the convicted convict necessarily has to languish in prison, which is harder to bear than any other type of incarceration.

Nathuram and Nana Apte were not exempt from any of the rules apply to convicted convicts. Even under such depressing and oppressive conditions in prison, the person condemned lives on whether she wants to or not. The person to be executed harbors some hope that perhaps his death penalty can be changed to another type of punishment minor, or perhaps annulled altogether and go free, who knows? So fooled by a deep hope, endure all the harassment and humiliation of the prison.

Nathuram, however, never harbored any hope, because he did not appeal against the death sentence ruling and the Superior Court had no reason to reconsider his condemns in that regard. Nana Apte was neither less brave nor less patient.

While we, the defendants, were kept in the special prison of Red Fort as prisoners of trial, Nathuram, Nana Apte and Savarkar used to have arguments about the sutras of Patanjali yoga.

In the contemporary circle of friends, Nana is known as someone given to luxurious lifestyle, while Nathuram for being ascetic, of course speaking in a sense a bit exaggerated.

Nana may have given herself a luxurious lifestyle, we can assume that for some time, but in his cell for the condemned he was master of himself and firm.

Nathuram and Apte were held in the convict cells of the Ambala Central Prison. About a week before the execution, the Central Government Ministry announced that the date for the execution of Nathuram and Apte it would be November 15, 1949. The relatives of the children were informed by telegraph convicted who could see them for the last time on November 14, 1949. The relatives who were from 30 to 35 gathered to have the last "Darshan" of both Nathuram and of Apte.

The meeting was sad at first on the part of the visitors, but in the end it was nice. One of the relatives asked:

> Well Nathuram, it is the custom to dip the ashes (remains) in the Ganga in Haridwar, in the Triveni Sangam (meeting the three rivers) in Prayagraj, or on the Gadavari in Nasik. How did you choose the river "Sindhu" for the immersion of your remains?

His response was immediate:

> It is the only river that has remained uncontaminated.

There was a great laugh. Everyone present knew that Gandhiji's remains could not sink into the "Sindhu". Nathuram even referred to it in paragraph 128 of his statement.

Relatives learned about Nathuram's Will. That was how his response evoked laughter. The conversation was in Maharati. The jailer, who was a refugee from Punjab, asked what was the fun. He was told the answer in Hindi and neither could he avoid laughing.

The meeting between Nana Apte and his wife, Champutai, was extremely touching. "Look", Nana said to her, "from tomorrow on you will have to cry, cry and cry! This brief moment has come to us to give us a good talk in private. Why don't we have a happy time?

The group returned very jubilant to see both convicts out of reach of the fear, even on the threshold of Death. They would be hanged the next morning. Karkare, Madan Lal and I went to see Nathuram and Nana again. We recite some chapters of the Bhagwat Gita, in particular II, and XI and XVIII, which were the that Nathuram liked best.

The jailers on duty chatted, chatted and chatted with them all night, claiming that they would not have a chance later. It was true. The Superintendent, jailers and staff generated affection for them for their moral foundation behind the act and for the high morals of the convicted convicts.

We went to see Nathuram and Nana again at sunrise. None of us he was sentimental or crestfallen with pain that time. They were happy while keep our composure. We were certainly not discouraged.

With the tender rays of the sun at 8 a.m., both Nathuram and Nana were ready to face the gallows with the undivided map of India, the colored flag saffron and a copy of the Bhagwat Gita in his hands. Apte was delighted to see the soft rays of the sun, and at the moment he exclaimed with joy, "Pandit, how lovely, what fascinating is the sunlight of this early morning"

"Oh! Heavens, " Nathuram replied equally enthusiastically, " it's almost always quite nice in Simla".

"Akhand Bharat Amar Rahe! " (Long live undivided India!) And, Vande Mataram'

(Here I bow to you, Oh Mother!) Were the heartbreaking slogans on her lips when they entered the execution chamber. Once inside it, and with the strings around their necks they both sang loudly:

Namaste Sada Vatsale Matribhume
Twaya Hindubhume Sukham Vardhitoham
Mahanmangale Punyabhume Twadarthe
Patatwesh Kayo Namaste, Namaste!'
Vande mataram
Translated into Spanish it means:
I bow down to you, oh, living Motherland, forever!
Raised by you I find myself in happiness,
O Land of the Hindus!
O most holy and blessed Earth, for your sake
Let this body fall! I bow to you, I bow to you
Forever and always!

Vande mataram

As soon as these words mixed with the atmosphere, the executioner pulled the bar of the planks beneath their feet and the two lives forever intermingled with the Five elements! The timing of the executioner's movement would also describe it as an act of nature, for it was so perfectly calculated that the planks They moved after the word "Vande" giving enough time for "Mataram" was pronounced before the rope took over.

I have come to the conclusion that revolutionaries have a spiritual philosophy own, which in my opinion is based on facing the gallows and staring without a blink at the eyes of Death itself.

The cremation took place inside the jail building. The day after the execution from Nathuram and Apte, when the visitors returned to the Ambala Railway Station For their return trip, the station was thronged with the local folks to see them off, and all the The courtyard resounded with the loud cries of "...... ki jai", as a gesture of sympathy. Nathuram made his "Testament", in which the last wish he expressed imposed on "The people" drop their ashes into the Indus (the Sindhu), only when that river belonged to the Indian national flag as an undivided and integral part of the nation: it may be after over a span of many years and after many generations! A copy of your Testament appears in the appendix.

That was the end of Nathuram V. Godse and Nana Apte, defendants 1 and 2. The others Defendants served their sentences, after which they were released.

❏

Profile of Nathuram Godse and the Rest of the Defendants

1. Nathuram Vinayak Godse, Defendant No. 1, was born on May 19, 1910 in Biramati, Poona District. It comes from the Chitpavan Brahmin community. The grandfather of Nathuram, that is, the father of his father, was a learned Brahmin named Vamanrao. Apart from agriculture he carried out the profession of the priesthood. His native people were Uksan.

Vamanrao had three daughters and a son, whom he named Vinayak, born in 1875. When Vinayak, in the last year of his school education, was seventeen years old, he married Godavari about 10 years old. Then her name changed to Lakshmi.

When he passed his exam to get out of school, he was hired at the Postal Department with a monthly salary of five rupees for the first three months, and then fifteen rupees. Lakshmi gave birth to a son in Baramati. It was on 19 May 1910. He was nicknamed "Nathu". This nickname was later changed to Nathuram. Nathuram began his primary education in Baramati. Your ceremony Graduation took place at Ram Mandir. Nathuram memorized a large part from "Selections of Marathi Poetry from the Middle Evo and the Nineteenth Century, Navaneeta."

Nathuram became interested in reading at an early age. He started reading the "Kesari", no because he understood its content, but simply for the love of reading. Naturally, that it was published about the achievement of independence influenced it indirectly and more forward, directly.

After passing the fourth grade of primary school he was taken to his aunt in Pune for your education in English. Nathuram's way of reasoning was completely rational, but that was the case until he grew up. During her childhood she was more sentimental than rational.

In every generation there is always an enthusiastic young man who takes great interest in social work and Nathuram was one of them.

While in Lonavala, a boy fell into a well and his mother and other women from cries and cries rose all around. At that moment, Nathuram and one of his friends were passing near. The well had steps. The little boy had not drowned. So Nathuram He immediately jumped into the well, took the boy, and climbed the steps up.

The child saved was of the Mahar caste, some said untouchable. Whatever were the reasons that led him to join the campaign against the castes from the heart, This must have been one of them.

Nathuram was, however, consciously alert to the political activities of the moment. One result of his political awareness was that his attention was diverted from his studies. At that time, when the Satyagraha movement accumulated momentum under the Gandhiji's leadership, he asked his father if he could join. This one told him that education it should take precedence over anything else.

Nathuram, who was studying at Nootan Marathi Vidyalaya, appeared for his matriculation exam. Meanwhile, his father was transferred to Ratnagiri in 1929- 30. This transfer was not only a revolutionary event in the life of Vinayakrao, but also in Nathuram's.

At that time Veer Savarkar lived in Ratnagiri. I was under restriction government and was prohibited from leaving the Ratnagiri district border, as well as writing, discuss or conference on political issues. People only knew Savarkar surreptitiously. By then he published his series of articles called "Mazi Janamthep" (My Banishment for Life), but in book format it was later banned and confiscated. Nathuram came to know the greatness of Veer Savarkar.

From time to time Nathuram heard from Veer Savarkar about his exploits. in London. He once brought home a copy of "War of Independence 1857" from Savarkar and used to read it at night. Nathuram gladly undertook the task of copying the written by Veer Savarkar. He was happy because of all the people he was the first to meet him.

Savarkar often gave him guidance on how to read and what to read. Nathuram began to participate in public meetings on political issues.

The Rashtriya Swayamsevak Sangh (RSS), founded by Dr. Hedgewar, with the intent on organizing Hindus, it was rapidly gaining popularity. Nathuram came to know about this organization.

The attitude of the Muslim community, as a whole, towards the struggle to obtain independence was clearly seen, even at that time, somewhat indifferent and even in blatantly hostile occasions.

A branch of the RSS was opened in Sangli headed by Shri Kashinathpant Limaye. Nathuram began to participate in the Sangh activities more assiduously. He soon came to head the academic department (as *"Baudhik Karyawaha"*).

In 1937, the Cooper-Jamnadas Ministry completely released Veer Savarkar. On the way to Bombay, he was congratulated in Kolhapur, Miraj, Sangli, Pune and elsewhere, and in each of them gave lectures. Nathuram started walking with Veer Savarkar at all parts, then began to realize how gigantic the task of organizing the Hindus to form a homogeneous whole, and also that the work of the Sangh (RSS) it required to be supplemented by an uprising in the political arena. His vision began to expand, and he felt that Sangli was a very small place for his activities. It was established in Pune.

In 1938, the Hindu Mahasabha decided to launch a campaign to eliminate the injustice towards the Hindus of the Haiderabad State so that they could obtain their legitimate rights. The name that was given to this was "Inarme resistance."

Nathuram led the first group of the peaceful resistance. Both he and his comrades were sentenced to one year in prison, in Haiderabad jail.

Nathuram decided to start a newspaper for the Hindu Mahasabha. It was "Agrani", some years later it was renamed "Hindu Rashtra". Bail was repeatedly required from this newspaper. After publication of its last issue of January 31, 1948, it went out of circulation.

The six to seven year period leading up to 1948 was a very busy one in the life of Nathuram, busy writing newspaper articles, speeches, traveling and various things strange things he had to do to handle the newspaper, and to make an inventory of which I would have to write a separate article. For the moment it should suffice to say that Nathauram devoted himself entirely to the work of the Hindu-Sangathan, that is to cause the solidarity of the Hindus.

Nathuram was peaceful and generous by nature. However, on the platform Politics gave free rein to his feelings, which at times seemed to reach the extreme limits of resistance, and yet he struggled to contain them.

Nathuram could skillfully play the harmonium. He played the flute equally well.

Nathuram was not unfamiliar with the activities initiated by Gandhiji to awakening the masses, he also did not disregard its importance. It would be enlightening to see under what mental state made the decision to assassinate him.

Those who regard the Gandhiji murder episode as a casual act of a person ready to shoot at the slightest provocation are ignorant, because they are victims innocent of propaganda.

Gandhiji, through the technique of his Satyagraha, communicated to the masses the true meaning of the words "the slavery of our country", "Swaraj", etc.

The rising generation at the height of Gandhiji's political career fed on the lively doses of the songs of independence from her lips.

Armed revolution was never Gandhiji's creed. But, the political consciousness of the people were so intense that they freely yelled *"Sardar Bhagat Singh ki jai"* as they came out in campaigns to awaken the masses.

It is true that many congressional leaders felt that Gandhiji's policy regarding the communal problem had been triggered, and therefore he had to withdraw from the active policy and should not intrude on national decisions.

Severe, of course, were the feelings of the refugees. Independence? To what cost? Such was the miserable condition in which they found themselves, for the very earth under their feet had literally slipped away without a shaking occurring. Waves and waves of Blood-soaked refugees returned to India every day.

Each displaced person was himself or herself a painful wound that actually had a voice. No newspaper could have been successful in airing discontent and outrage and in overloading the entire atmosphere with intense feeling, even with the intention, as scathing and on such a vast scale as every sign and word of the countless voices of the refugees.

Countless people uttered bitter curses, not only in their private homes, but in public places; it was because of Gandhiji that they had lost their houses and homes so they shouldn't live. However, the idea of killing Gandhiji was, by itself, much more painful and disgusting.

A dose of potent poison dripped out. Can you imagine how difficult it was for Nathuram deciding to assassinate Gandhiji as a terrible duty and an ominous obligation?

Stand in front of the world with all past life completely reduced to dust and To suffer all sorts of indignity, contempt, and humiliation from it was most appalling and unbearable than self-immolation. So one can see quite well that this murder it was not an act of caprice of a inveterate monomaniac shooting at will.

It is obvious, therefore, that there must have been a powerful cause or a chain of them which incited the mind of Nahuram to the point of denying Gandhiji earthly existence, and as a consequence of this, himself.

Nathuram had at least the satisfaction that he was not considered a maniac. suffering from some morbidity.

Nathuram told us about the incident:

> He had a gun in his hand. I fired the bullets. No one could tell with trust he hadn't fired a few more bullets. If some police would have fired a bullet at me at that moment, it would certainly have justified.

> As soon as I fired the bullets, I raised my hand that I was holding the gun and yelled "Police, Police." Half a minute passed, still no one dared to approach. Every moment increased the tension in my mind and I became absolutely restless. I think I was getting excited.

> At that time I was not at all aware of whether or not someone was going to hit me, I did not have in mind the slightest thought of protecting myself of the blows if someone offered to beat me. Today I can interpret my mental condition as it was at the time. I was prepared for face any consequences for the act of assassinating Gandhiji. Not alone I wanted no one to file three charges against me. First i didn't want Let no one imply that I tried to run away Half a minute later I screamed again "Police, Police." I could see quite well, standing right in front of me at uniformed policeman, and did not dare to step forward to arrest me. If I had thrown my gun (to dispel his fear), that action of mine would be would have taken in the sense that he prepared an escape for me defending. Naturally, I didn't want such a claim to be made against me. AND, he was perplexed as to how to convince the police that he wanted surrender, weapon in hand, to them.

> He didn't want to hurt anyone else by mistake. That is why I kept waiting for the policeman to approach, with my hand up holding the gun. If I had kept my hand down playing with the pistol, even inadvertently, there would certainly have been witnesses They will declare that I pointed the gun at them.

> I started looking around and probably found myself with the gaze of Amarnath or that of the so-called soldier.

He seemed convinced of the sincerity in my eyes and held my wrist elevated. Must have felt the total absence of resistance in it. The tension in my mind soon disappeared and I let out a sigh of relief. Still another man followed, who seized of my weapon, which I dropped without any resistance.

And, after that, people came up to me and surrounded me. Some me they beat with their hands. The police were stupid enough to allow the pistol to change hands to satisfy the curious.

Someone from the crowd pointed her at me, saying "With this same gun I'll kill you ". Calmly but loud enough so that my words were audible to him, even in that tumultuous noise, I replied, "With pleasure. Ahead. But, it doesn't seem like you have knowledge of how to handle a gun. Look, the safety is on.

Even if luckily he received the slightest tug, he would probably kill someone plus. Remember, there are some bullets in it. " Then I asked the officer nearest police officer to take the gun into his custody, reminding him to the safety was on and there was every probability that the man kill someone else instead of me. The officer immediately took possession of that pistol, he closed the safety and put it in his pocket. I arrived at the gates of Birla Bhavan around five to ten in the afternoon. The guards there watched very closely the people who He entered the meeting to pray. I expected the greatest danger from these guards. So, taking the utmost precaution to pretend that belonged to a group of four or five people entering, I managed to enter to the Birla Bhavan. Again I felt that the cops coming and going had, so to speak, focused their eyes on me, because the ground to pray it was still almost empty. So I rushed in as quickly as possible where people were standing in greater numbers and I placed myself there.

About five minutes past five I saw Gandhiji and his Entourage leave the room and approach the floor to pray. I went and stood among a group of people near the place where you would ascend the steps down to the ground for prayer.

Gandhiji ascended the steps and advanced five or six steps, his hands resting on the shoulders of two girls.

I opened the safety of the gun inside the same bag. There was already observed that he could have the scope he wanted despite the people around Gandhiji.

I needed about three more seconds to get two steps ahead, stand in front of Gandhiji, take the gun out of my pocket, and ask him reverence for any useful service they have rendered to the country and the sacrifice you have made during your life on this.

Of the two girls accompanying Gandhiji, one was quite close to him and I feared that I might get hurt in the attempt. So deciding what to do to avoid that eventuality, I moved forward and uttering the words "Namaste" (I bow to you) I bowed to Gandhiji holding the gun with his hands. Moving one step closer to him front I pushed the girl aside.

In the next fraction of a second the shots were fired. Weak As it was, Gandhiji collapsed on the ground dead almost instantly, with the "Ah!"[1] weaker that emerged from deep within her lungs.

The indestructible, fireproof and sub-changeable soul that also unable to dry himself off, he quickly left the body and faded into the elements and I entered my Samadhi in life (undead).

Nathuram had already decided from the very beginning of the trial not to allow his lawyer question the witnesses presented to testify regarding the events of January 30, of course, to the extent of what they said about that event.

Many eyewitnesses were examined. Nathuram admired his enthusiasm, but had pity for his "honesty". Everyone wanted credit for apprehending him. Your statements they were inconsistent and contradictory with each other.

---

1   The words "Hey Ram, Hey Ram and Hey Ram" were a fiction of the imagination of the Government of that then and they attributed them to gain the Hindu sentiment.

Nathuram had a seven-round automatic pistol with him. He pulled the trigger just once. Two or three bullets came out.

Lieutenant Colonel BL Taneja, Suppl. Civil Surgeon, Irwin Hospital, New Delhi, gave during the course of his evidence the description of five wounds on the body of Gandhiji, and said that in his opinion the bullets from the pistol caused the death. Neither to him he was questioned.

The East Punjab High Court saw his theoretical stance on Nathuram. Of the appellants, the honorable Members said that according to their judgment:

> Nathuram V. Godse has not challenged his sentence under Section 302 of the Indian Penal Code for the crime of assassinating Mahatma Gandhi on 30 January 1948, nor has he appealed the death sentence that was handed down to him to that crime. You have limited your appeal as well as your arguments in the court, he argued his appeal personally, I must say skillfully conspicuous, evidencing a mastery of the facts that would have given him credit to any attorney, solely for the other charges against you.

In an argument regarding the January 20 incident, Judge Acchru Ram said:

> We have seen enough of Nathuram for the period of more than five weeks while we hear your appeals and particularly during the eight or nine days while he argued his own case, and I can't imagine that a man of his caliber has even considered the idea (of staying behind).

The judges evidently realized that this homicide had been an unfortunate consequence of the situation that prevailed at that time in the country. The court Lahore city superior had to flee for safety and became a refugee as Hindus from that city and state and were forcibly removed from the rest of the indian territory. If sentencing Nathuram to death was doing justice to the people, then so was the fair evaluation of his feelings.

Coffee was his favorite drink. He has never had tea since his teens. While in the prison cell once told the jailer in a joking way, "I don't care about the Gallow; but I must have a cup of coffee before the execution. " The way you climbed to the rope and the words he spoke have been described above. Such was the man called Nathuram V. Godse.

Lifeforms are strange, because of Nathuram's post-assassination movements V. Godse and being what was his position before the Court, the Government, for its own political benefit, even awarded a Kirti Chakra in a prog. Raj Singh for having "Apprehended" Godse. The High Court found that Nathuram made no attempt some for fleeing.

2. Narayan Dattatraya Apte (Defendant No. 2) was born in 1911. Generally known like Nana. Nana's four brothers, Balwant, Vishnu, Madhav and Manohar, were engaged in their own separate professions. Manohar was also in the foreigner for higher education.

After earning her Bachelor of Science degree, Nana accepted a job as teacher in Atmednagar. During his stay at Atmednagar, he married the daughter of Shri Phadtare.

At Atmednagar, his innate ability and deep interest in teaching attracted pupillos to the private teachings that he imparted. He appeared for his examination for the Bachelor of Theology and obtained his degree.

Endowed with a fair complexion and sculpted features, but with a body with a complexion a little soft, the always smiling Nana was known in her circle of friends for being eminently suitable for a female role.

Faith and loyalty to Hinduism are inherent, at least in families learned from Maharashtra. So Nana was also raised under these domestic influences. traditional.

Nana's ability and dexterity to organize developed rapidly, as his contact with Nathuram matured through the Hindu Mahasabha sessions and gradually they both came to realize that the other possessed some strange qualities. Consequently, in early 1944 they both planned to start a journal, called "Agrani". Nana became the director of the newspaper, while Nathuram, its editor. This editor-editor relationship was firm until the end.

The Government of that time used to be exasperated with the policy of the Hindu Mahasabha to foster loyalty to Hindutwa among Hindus, because the Ministries of Congress followed the policy of appeasement of Muslims. They sued "Agrani" security deposits in quick succession.

While Gandhiji stayed in Panchagani, a group of about twenty-five young led by Nana organized a protest against Gandhiji's policies on July 1944.

Nana planned and executed another such demonstration before Gandhiji when he was in the street sweepers' colony in Delhi, with the aim of personally telling him not to make any donation to Muslims at the expense of Hindus, as such a donation was not to appease them; not to accept the partition of India; and learn a lesson from the massacre of the Hindus in Noakhali. All of Gandhiji's previous promises they proved futile and the land was divided.

Nana Apte made a separate will in which she stated, among other things, the desire to submerge his remains in the Sindhu River, just as Nathuram had done. On one occasion Nana told me, "Look, Gopal, from the deceased's point of view, It is absolutely immaterial how his body or his ashes are disposed of! But the Survivors of the deceased are eager to honor their feelings. We don't have a faith blind in our manuscripts. True, we habitually submerge our mortal remains on the Ganga. But don't we consider all the rivers of India equally sacred? Remember, our death is of a political nature, more particularly national; such as it is natural that we should harbor feelings of loyalty to our nation. But now that you have brought this question before us, I must answer it with satisfaction. There are two wounds that constantly afflict our hearts.

This new-born state of Pakistan is a parasitic herb that has grown spitefully in the land of the Hindus sucking their life current, Nana uttered with passionate indignation. As soon as you received the sustenance of independence and separate existence, began to inflict insults to the rest of India. We have restricted our observation to things that concern us, because that is our limit. May i ask which of all nations have insulted Gandhiji after his death?

Which one?

None other than Pakistan! Do you remember the message of condolence sent by Jinnah?

Yes, pretty good. A leader of the Hindus has passed away.

Isn't that a great insult to Gandhiji? How?

Wasn't it Jinnah's duty to show gratitude for the man, at least after death, who throughout his life suppressed aspirations just to encourage through their condescension and concessions the projects aggressive and fissioning Muslims in India in vain hope to carry out a Hindu-Muslim unity? If I had called, and yes called Gandhiji to be such a leader before the birth of Pakistan, not it would have been an insult to him. Well, it would have looked like a ruse Jinnah's politician to reach his end. That is why we wish formally that only after the state where Gandhiji was insulted as "Hindu" submits to our control with the entire Indus River, the Sindhu, who waters the territories under the power of India, our remains be immersed in it, the sacred river of us, ours from the most ancient from the past.

Shri Shreeprakash was the then Indian High Commissioner in Pakistan, who complained to tears in his voice that the Government of Pakistan did not allow the immersion of the ashes of Gandhiji on the Indus River. But, the submergence of Gandhiji's ashes in the Indus River was purely a matter of sentiment, and more particularly one of Hindu sentiment. So how could they tolerate the holy water of a holy river in their holy land contaminated with the ashes of a Hindu?

"We fondly hope," Nana continued, "that our government will preserve a urn containing Gandhiji's ashes to be submerged in the Indus River when it was possible to do so. But, we swallowed that insulting refusal from Pakistan in a quite shy".

Nana told his wife, Soubhagyavati Champutai, "If you believe in the immortality of the soul, then you are and will remain Soubhagyavati even after my death! Change of place in society wearing your external symbols of your Soubhagya.[2] Soubhagyavati works as a teacher in the kindergarten run by Rani Lakshmibai Smarak Mandal.

3. Vishnu Ramkrishna Karkare (Defendant No. 3) had a boarding house and accommodation in Ahmednagar. He was an active worker. When Noakhali in Bengal (now in Bangala Desh) became the slaughterhouse of the Hindus there, Karkare, with a group out of ten, he went there to mobilize Hindus and take a militant stance in their defense. He raised a number of refuge camps under the Hindu Mahasabha banner. This was in 1946-47. Vishnu Karkare continued his business in Ahmednagar until he died of a heart attack on April 6, 1974. His wife runs the business.

4. Madan Lal Pahwa (Defendant No. 4), who blew up the gunpowder plate, he was a refugee. He witnessed the terrible events of massacre, looting and burning caused. Carvans, continuous miles in length and comprising hundreds of thousands of Humans expelled from their homes and homes, were on their way to truncated India. Madan Lal recounted his moving sufferings in his statement before the Court.

Madan Lal, who married after his release, manages purchases and sales for some paper mills in Bombay.

5. Shankar Kistaiya (Defendant No. 5) served Digambar Badge, the whistleblower (as personal / domestic servant). He died within a few years of his acquittal.

6. I, (**Gopal Godse** and author of this book) was defendant No. 6. I was charged with conspiracy under the allegation that I was present at Birla House on January 20. I was convicted of complicity and sentenced to life in exile.

---

2   "Soubhagyavati" precedes the name of a married Hindu woman whose husband is alive. Mangala Sootra, a kind of necklace with a particular design, around the neck, and a Kumkum Tilak, that is, a red mark on the forehead they are carried by said woman, usually in Maharashtra and in the south.

I was born on June 20, 1920. Of the four brothers I am the third. In that So our father was sent to Khed (now Rajgurnagar) in the Pune district. Govind he was the youngest. He was born two years later in Telegaon, in the Pune district. The eldest was our sister Mathura. There was another older than me by the name of Shanta. Both no longer is it so.

My primary education started in Karjat in the Raigarh district, and continued in Ratnagiri. After the retirement of our father, we settled in Sangli. I approved my registration.

I was a volunteer for the Hindu organization RSS Simultaneously also I worked for the Hindu Mahasabha, but without enrolling as a member.

World War II had broken out. I joined the Defense Services as a kerchief in the Indian Army Artillery Corps in 1940. I opted for service from the front, and served in Iraq and Iran until April 1944.

When I returned I was sent to Kirkee and then I got married. My wife's name is Sindhu. We have two daughters, one named Vidyullata and the other Asilata. When i was arrested In February 1948, the oldest was two years old and the youngest just three or four months old. Sindhu alone she assumed the responsibilities of both father and mother and raised the daughters. My older brother, Dattatraya (died 9/10/1990), who was next to Nathuram, ran an engineering workshop called "Udyam Engineering", where Sindhu also worked. Initially he lived with the same family, but later he built a home apart for her and her daughters. Later he also started a small workshop of hers called "Pratap Engineering".

It is a tradition of history that when a revolutionary is imprisoned, his relatives and dependents must suffer unspeakable hardships of various kinds.

Shri Dattatraya, turned his "Udyam Engineering" into a society of limited liability just before Gandhiji's assassination. While Shri Dattatraya was under arrest, his wife, Smt. Sarojini attended to household affairs fairly skill.

While the Goa liberation movement was in full swing, several young people bravely participated in it. In a group of seven was a boy named Narayan Dattatraya Kulkarni. This adorable boy had something that constantly pricked in her mind, unfortunately she did not receive maternal affection as she grew up. Sindhu compensated for this desire for maternal love; and today Nana lives with us as ours Foster son. The report of my period in jail and life after release I give it more ahead.

7. Digambar Badge was originally defendant No. 7, but became so officer in the informer. No. 7 was assigned to Savarkar. Digambar Badge was a Sangha-Hindu and an arms dealer. He believed that Hindus should arm themselves in the groups in which they were a minority and be able to retaliate in the event of an attack of Muslims. The prosecuting party stated that it was Badge who supplied the plate gunpowder cotton lit by Madan Lal. A hand grenade was also recovered by Madan Lal. More ammunition was recovered from Badge.

Upon his release from custody, Digambar Badge was served in the Police department. Since then he retired.

8. Of the nine defendants brought before the Special Court, Red Fort, Delhi, in the Gandhiji's murder case, Swatantryaveer Vinayak Damodar Savarkar was originally ordered as Defendant No. 8. As mentioned above, on May 1948 all the accused appeared before the Special Court for the first time. Digambar Ramchandra Badge, defendant No. 7, turned whistleblower. So it was removed officially off the bench and consequently the numbers of the other defendants went up. Savarkar, therefore, became defendant No. 7.

Vinayak Damodar Savarkar was born on 05.28.1883 in Bhagoor, a town near Nasik, a district of the city in Maharashtra. Nasik is famous for its importance religious. As Savarkar's birthplace, Bhagoor also became an altar for the devotees of Swaraj. Vinayak's father, Damodar, was an innkeeper in the sense humble. Vinayak had an older brother named Ganesh and a younger brother named Narayan. Vinayak's mother, Radha, was a lady of the home.

Vinayak had a sharp memory. He could recite verses with little effort. This it formed the basis for him to compose poetry in subsequent years. From the very childhood, Vinayak showed a tendency to organize children his age and attract them to programs to the liberation of the country from the British yoke. He called the groups *"Mitra Mela"* (meeting of friends).

In Bhagoor there was a deity of the goddess Bhagwati who had eight arms. Vinayak, who was barely fifteen years old, promised before the goddess that he would wear a fight the British to defeat them and that in the course of it he would fight until he spilled the last drop of his blood.

Vinayak had his primary education at Bhagoor and then Nasik. After graduating he went to Pune and joined the Ferguson College. He continued his organizational work in Pune also among the college students. Sometimes he consulted the leaders of then such as Lokmanya Tilak and Shivram Mahadev Paranjpe.

In 1906, Vinayak organized a foreign clothing bonfire in Pune. It was the first act of open revolt against the purchase of British goods.

Vinayak graduated from Ferguson College. He wanted to go to England to study the law and become a lawyer. Pandit Shaymjee Krishna Varma promoted a scholarship. Lokmanya Tilak recommended Vinayak for this one.

Vinayak came to England and here he had a wider field to sow the patriotism in the youth of different provinces. He also wrote for "Kal", a magazine by SM Paranjpe. The language of his news was fiery, yet cleverly written.

Madan Lal Dhingra, the young man who shot and killed Corzen Waily on June 22, 1909, he was sentenced to death. The statement found in Madan Lal's pocket Dhigra was suppressed by the police. Savarkar ordered its publication in a newspaper one day before the execution of Dhingra, that is, on

August 16, 1909. The title was "Reto", meaning that the police should talk about whether or not this was Madan Lal's statement Dhingra that had been seized after his arrest. Madan Lal Dhingra was executed in the Bristol prison on August 17, 1909.

In India, Anant Kanhere, a 17-year-old boy, murdered the Nasik, Mr. Jackson, on December 22, 1909. Savarkar was arrested in London on 13.3.1910 and was brought to India to be tried in this case. On the road, in Marseilles, France, Savarkar jumped off the ship and reached the shore, but was apprehended and taken from back to the ship.

Savarkar, along with thirty-four others, was charged with sedition. The 24.12.1910 was sentenced to exile for life. He was also charged for participation in the case of the murder of Jackson. On January 30, 1911, he was again sentenced to life in exile. I know ordered the sentences to be executed consecutively.

Savarkar was transported to Andamans (Kala Pani) on 1.7.1911, where he remained for ten years. In May 1921, Vinayak was brought back and housed in the Jail of Yeravada (Pune) about three years. On 6.1.1924, he traveled to Vinayak to Ratnagiri and was he stayed there with some restrictions until 1937 when he was finally released. From the day Savarkar was released from his detention in Ratnagiri, the Savarkarism and Gandhism had to confront openly. In addition to its mission life to achieve national independence, Savarkar now had to undertake another program to refute this unbalanced principle of nonviolence, which made noise in people's ears day after day, and the constructive aspect of this program was the work of organize Hindus, "Hindu Sangha".

The Hindu Mahasabha was a new contender in the field of Indian politics. I know elected Savarkar as President of the Hindu Mahasabha to preside over the session in Karnavati, meaning Ahmedabad, held in December 1937.

Savarkar had a caution. His call to young Indians to join the British army with the prospect of learning the techniques of war and weapons modern and not miss the opportunity sent by

God to be worthy for war and that they equip themselves with weapons, giving the opportune time to teach them against who would use these weapons, Congress willfully and maliciously distorted and then ridiculed with his well-organized propaganda system, which could publish very easily in a perverse way that the Hindu Mahasabha was anti-independence, revisionist and retrograde.

Early in 1942, at his home in Kanpur, Savarkar predicted that Congress He was going to divide the country and he warned the nation about it. And, five years later, it became true.

On August 15, 1947, independence was achieved. To recognize this victory, Veer Savarkar hoisted the pan-Hindu flag of the Hindu Mahasabha on top of his home, and also accepted the national flag with three colors and the Ashok Chakra in the center.

Veer Savarkar thought that since the Hindus were going to be expelled from the territory now known as Pakistan, Muslims from the rest of India were not to be prevented let them go to Pakistan which was their own creation. He was alert to events and was prophetic in his words. Vinayak Damodar Savarkar became known as Swatantrya Veer for his incessant efforts and suffering, his audacity and courage, his direction and advice to achieve Sawaraj.

Gandhiji was assassinated on 1/30/1948. The next day, a series of arrests began on a large scale of Hindu leaders and others. In the next few weeks, he was arrested near 10,000 people under the Preventive Detention Act. All of them were only Hindus. Savarkar's house was searched. Files and papers were seized for scrutiny. While Savarkar remained in pre-trial detention, he was kept under surveillance of your family, friends and associates.

One can safely infer that before independence, the Government of the Congress under the leadership of Pandit Nehru was examining how to ensure its survival in the power after her. Following the murder, which was just over five months after the independence, they were quick to gauge general Hindu sentiment, so they had to proceed with your task of ensuring their survival a little more carefully, and for this they considered that it was necessary to do two things:

(i) Divide the Hindus into caste lineages.

(ii) Appease the Muslims.

And, Savarkar always had a firm predicament that there could be no distinction between a Hindu and another by caste lineage and that there should be no appeasement of any section or community for political gains. Therefore, instead of granting it a "Award" to Veer Savarkar for his contribution to the independence of India, they decided implicate him in the Gandhiji murder case so that his pending arrest trial coupled with a diversion of energies with respect to the defense of the case, and could give them a much needed rest to carry out his aforementioned objective of dividing the Hindus in caste lineages, appease the Muslims, and further test and introduce their confidants (sycophants) as apparent Hindu leaders, the purpose being change in some way or another the Hindu approach from one man to various people of his own installation.

Since the meticulous search of the papers seized in Veer's house Savarkar (documents and correspondence dating from 1938 and amounting to 143 files with 10,000 papers), and other investigations revealed nothing incriminating, They used the third degree method against Badge, promising forgiveness and the result was that the police had a statement from Badge implicating Savarkar. Then by Consequently, Savarkar's arrest went from being one under the Pretrial Detention Act to one one in which he was charged in the Gandhiji murder case. The trial took time and effort, all this while Savarkar remained in prison. A year later, on the day of sentence arrived. Savarkar was acquitted.

An immense crowd of people gathered to greet Savarkar out of Red Fort. The exonerated Savarkar was leaving Red Fort.

The crowd was visibly excited, and like an ocean embraced Savarkar with the piercing cries of:

Swatantrya Lakshmi Ki Jai!
(Victory of the Goddess of Liberty)
Akhand Bharat Amar Rahe!
(Long live the undivided India)
Swatantryaveer Savarkar Ki Jai!
(Victory to Swa. Savarkar)

Veer Savarkar inaugurated the Calcutta Session of the Hindu Mahasabha after his liberation in the year 1949, in which Shri NB Khare was elected as President. After 1950, his sick condition prevented him from participating in public functions. Only rarely he conducted public meetings.

In 1957, in Delhi, he led the meeting to mark the centenary of the first War of Independence, fought in 1857. His speech was moving. Said:

> *You have followed me so far despite the fact that in return they received no honor or welfare. What they received in return was imprisonment, hanging, hatred from the people and curses from the secularists. And yet they still did not give up on this path and followed it to the end in full force. This spirit of his will certainly lead the Hindus to obtain your cultural independence.*

In subsequent years he gave lectures on Hindu History. Have been compiled as "Six Glorious Ages."

People congratulated Veer Savarkar in the year 1960, and named the occasion as "Mrityunjaya Din." If two consecutive punishments of banishment for life were to be carried out in his case, he was going to see the free world in that year. How Savarkar survived the year of programmed freedom, the occasion was called "Mrityunjaya" (who has dominated the deity of Death).

In early February 1966, when he was in his 83rd year, Savarkar decided that the soul had to get rid of the human body. He gave up food and confined himself to meditation. Prior to that, he wrote:

146

I have done everything possible with my humble strength for the good of my people, country. However, life has its own limitation. When the limbs can no longer be burdened with any task, surrender to Nature is the only honorable way. Let me be free now from the wrapping of the body that I possess.

Veer Savarkar died on February 26, 1966, in Bombay, ironically, after suffering the rigors of sentencing and detention both during British rule as well as when India was free. His fault:

He fought for the independence of India, opposed vivisection and separatists, urged for the just rights of Hindus, and was against of the division of the Hindus into caste lineage.

Many of his statements were compiled into a book by Shri GM Joshi and Balarao Savarkar. This is called "Historical Declarations by VD Savarkar".

One more thing about him. The fight for freedom was not a single effort man. It was the collective effort of thousands, and millions who were behind those Thousands. Savarkar was one of them. He is, however, in a more fortunate sense, for his soul has been saved from the outrage of false claims of today's politicians to give credit for what their sacrifices were. Sad to see that the credit for the sacrifice made by many genuine national patriotic figures be it Bhagat Singh, Uttam Chand, Madan Lal Dhingra, Khudi Ram, rash Behari or even Subhash Chandra Bose, who were not only patriots in the true sense, but men of values and principles, it is claimed and used by today's politicians to project themselves as heirs by his noble legacy. They orchestrate distorted propaganda and false trades enjoying their reflected glory and seeking to present itself as a fragment of the same block, before a nation that has been a calculated victim of little education and social divisions.

It is because Savarkar was so well known and his writings so profuse, that his contributions have been saved from such misuse. The day he was incarcerated and the day that he was released, or even the anniversaries of his birth and death, pass without sponsorship of public gatherings led by politicians wearing Gandhi caps, and followed by great coverage on TV/ Doordarshan and radio. At least this ensures that your soul rests in peace.

9. Dr. Dattatraya Sadashiv Parchure (Defendant No. 9) was a qualified physician. He was practicing in Gwalior. He was a skilled organizer. He faced the attacks of Muslims with counter attacks. He was implicated on the charge that Nathuram obtained the pistol from him. I know got a confession from him under pressure. The Superior Court acquitted him. Got married and he remained in his own home with his family. She died in 1986.

There were three more defendants cited by the prosecution. They were **Ganghadar Dandavate, Ganghadar Jadhao and Surya Dev Sharma,** all from Gwalior. They were declared fugitives. its Prosecution depended on the conviction of Dr. Parchure. The Superior Court acquitted the Dr. Parchure on June 22, 1949. After that, the three surrendered to the police, the which presented them before the local Magistrate who excused them from any accusation. Ganghadar Dandavate is gone. Ganghadar Jadhao remains in Nagpur. Surya Dev Sharma is located in Dattiya (MP). He was returned to the Madya Pradesh Assembly twice.

❏

The Period in Prison

While the matter was before the High Court and until the execution of Nathram and Apte, we remained in the Ambala Prison. Following the execution of Nathuram and Apte, Karkare and I was taken to Nasik Highway Central Prison in a cage cart by separate called the prisoner cart. We arrived at Nasik Central Prison on May 19, 1950.

The country's rationing system also affected the food served in prison.

Red jawar, which is of much inferior quality, and a runny paste were continually served made from the same jawar flour. Dal (legumes) and vegetables were served alternately as an appetizer along with the jawar bread. As a complementary food, they sometimes served a hodgepodge of cereals. Fourteen meals a week was the calendar, one of the which consisted of rice and one of wheat flatbreads.

By the method of our labor and the progress we made in it and the skill we we showed when executing the works, the officers felt that we should be used in some productive activity. It was decided to start a soap factory in Nasik Prison. It began on August 19, 1955.

Still later, an ink factory run at Thane Jail moved to the Nasik prison after a full deliberation of about a year and a half. Is factory also started in the same room No. 1.

The cases of long-term prisoners are presented for consideration before the Advisory Board. If in the meantime a prisoner is about to complete his fourteen years of stay in prison, the question of presenting the case for reconsideration after one or two years does not arise. In 1954, our cases were brought before the Advisory

Council by Norm, and was directed to re-submit after two years. In 1956, again they were postponed for another year.

On the first Republic Day of India we were given as part of amnesty generally a 40-day remission, which could not be reversed. We were given remission every year for good behavior. Referral for the extra work that we dedicate from time to time and whenever we were offered the option to choose between money or remittance, invariably we opted for referral. Although there is a rule that the total referral period does not should exceed one third of the total sentence period, and that if it did, it would have to be specially sanctioned by the Government; the remission granted as a general amnesty was an exception to this rule.

Meanwhile, on December 16, 1956, Karkare was medically examined, because for the previous seven or eight days he had shown signs of suffering from tuberculosis. While I was under sentence I donated blood seven times. For each donation of blood I was granted a remission of ten days. Twice I donated blood and asked for the remission. On five other occasions I donated blood as a simple "donation". But Jail Superintendent failed to honor his written remission guarantee of twenty days of sentence, only aimed at the Government.

On April 11, 1957 we received the decision in the report on our sentence fourteen-year-old, who said that the question of our liberation would be put up for consideration after the completion of fifteen years of stay. It was truly a devastating blow to that was given to us. This certainly did not accord with any procedure of the Code of Prison in force at that time.

The government can be proud of how they easily fooled a convict in the case of the murder of Gandhiji when exercising his authority, how he was mocked, how they took revenge by causing him mental anguish, how they were cruel to him. No one had the courage to suggest that constant repression of this type was inhumane. Perhaps they feared that if they gave their opinion in a clear and courageous way, they could be accused with having something to do with the conspiracy to assassinate Gandhiji.

My parents, exhausted with age and afflicted with worries, came to understand, by this decision of the Government, that they were not destined to see in their lives that so quickly they were finishing Gopal free from prison.

My parents once again came to see me at Nasik Central Prison for the last time. My mother, bent over with age, could not climb the steps upright; I almost know he crouched down to them. My mother became a mental wreck and fell to the bed when she reached House. He died on May 6, 1957. My father also died before more months.

The decision about my release was received, rather, how long I do not know It would set me free and for a few days I lost all my peace of mind. I only knew one thing, that I was he had done injustice and that the court was an institution to put an end to him.

I decided to defend my own case and in December 1957 I sent my first petition to Superior Court. My efforts to bring justice to the Superior Court were as an exercise in copying letters to improve the handwriting. This went on continuously and I he resisted all these defeats. During the seven years from December 1957 to August 1964, I wrote no less than twenty-two petitions to the Superior Court.

It was impossible for me to hire a lawyer. Sometimes I did consult some defense attorneys, but when they saw that the Superior Court had rejected several of my requests did not have the courage to argue the case. The decision of the Court was that as Section 401 Cr.PC authorized the Government to exercise the power of clemency, only he could free the prisoner subjected to life imprisonment.

My eighth request was heard on November 14, 1960. On January 12, 1961 the decision was released. While defining the sentence, the judges had confident in a decision given by the Privy Council thirty years ago. This decision was that there was no difference between "proscription" and "imprisonment", the latter being another name for the former, and hence it was exactly the same if the prisoner was sent to Andaman Jail or if he was kept in any prison in India. The court Superior accepted this ruling as a standard one and of sufficient weight to depend on it, and therefore Consequently, the judges on the stand did not delve. But, the Superior Court was a He went a step further by saying that "banishment for life" or "perpetual imprisonment" should be treated prima facie as banning or imprisonment altogether for the period remaining of the natural life of the convicted person. The crux of the decision was that as no one knew the exact day of the prisoner's death, it was not possible to deduce remission of her, and therefore, no dispute over the completion of the sentence, including the referral could take place. I decided to approach the Superior Court again.

I started writing a new petition discussing all matters relevant to, and having to do with, my contest, in particular the origin and implementation of, and the subsequent changes made to, death sentences, life exiles, imprisonment, life imprisonment, rigorous imprisonment, and simple imprisonment and so on, etc. and the utility of New South Wales in Australia, and the Andamans for the banishment of convicts, the prevailing criminal slavery centuries ago, the origin of the practice of granting referral, and its objective, trends criminals of humanity, origin and practice of holding prisons by governments, defects in thinking about the Privy Council, and discrepancies in the observations made by the Superior Court, etc. So I decided to send my request as a thesis under the title, Does a convict have to die in prison under Indian law? My request had extended up to 175 pages. It was presented to the Superior Court on October 28, 1961, numbered 16 of 1962 and rejected after that.

I was transferred from Nasik to Aurangabad Jail on January 20, 1962. My wife wrote to me in response on August 16, 1962.

I really believe, Gopal, that we too are meant to enjoy of the very happiness of salvation one of these days. But, we are still

152

for filling the measure of sufferings, humiliations, contempt, agonies mental and the anguish of complete separation until the moment of salvation come.

So soar to the top again! It is quite normal for a man in your situation is discouraged by the thought that all your efforts have been in vain. Did scientists give up on their attempts and remained motionless because they had to meet the failure in all his experiments to extract oil from the stones?

Even if the whole world turned its back on you, it's sure that I I will stay behind you, why, just by your side! Let's try it once plus.

I had served fifteen years of my sentence, not counting the remission period of February 1964. Still hemmed in on all sides and in a state of total mental distraction, I went ahead with my appeals to the Superior Court quite relentlessly. Firm a statement on 14.8.1964. I was presented to the Superior Court on 9/28/1964. I know discussed the matter in court for twenty minutes. They made the unanimous decision to ask the Government to appear at the preliminary hearing. The case was postponed to 19.10.1964.

It was Saturday, October 10, 1964. It was reported that the then Minister of the India, Shri Gulzarilal Nanda, would visit the Delhi Jail, to address the prisoner, who would be convened in the outdoor classroom.

After seeing one or two divisions of the jail, Shri Nanda asked for me. By the afternoon I was taken to the office. *What will you do after you are released?* Shri asked Nanda. I replied: *The question does not arise until today. But, if for something I was freed, would enter politics. I wish him well.* Shri Nanda said, and our meeting ended.

Tuesday 10/13/1964 arrived and our cells were opened. Little passed time when a jailer came and stood in front of me.

The order for their release has arrived. Pack your things. It will let you out before seven thirty.

The Superintendent granted me a hearing. I signed everything necessary in the book of registry. An order of banishment was issued. My luggage was inspected and maintained outside. I came out of jail with premature old age on my shoulders and breathed the first mass free air. Karkare and Madan were also released from their respective prisons.

I took the Dahradun Express and went to Pune via Kalyan. My people received me in Kalyan.

As I was greeted with the pancharetis (five ghee lamps commonly used for greetings) my heart choked with excitement. I didnt try stop them, but rather allowed my tears of excitement to roll down my cheeks. Was there no one who approached me affectionately about it? I felt a hunger insatiable for it.

Three of the older members of my family who could speak about it for their own right had already passed away. My mother, my father, and Nathuram! At the time of remembering them I went in and bowed in front of their photographs.

On 10/19/1964 I attended the Supreme Court. My request was carried out in court. I stood up. The judges had read my new appendix. The court did not find the need to consider the original request since the release had been effected, and the they interpreted it as unsuccessful.

❑

Life after Liberation

There was a large gap of about seventeen years, from February 1948 to September 1964. I entered the free world again. I assumed that the role of incarceration in my life had finished forever.

But it was not like that. My friends had welcomed me, and they organized a small ceremony. The late GV Ketkar, then editor of Tarun Bharat, a Marathi daily, he was the main guest. In his speech he said that he had tried to dissuade Nathuram from his thought of assassinating Gandhiji.

His statement resulted in biased articles. Consequently, we were made Karkare and myself along with ten others including Shri Ketkar under the Act of Defense of India that prevailed back then. We both suffered years of imprisonment without charge.

Due to my participation in the Gandhiji murder episode, I felt it had become a page in contemporary history. The story had been hidden by hypocritical rulers. It was for me that, as a page in history, I had to expose myself to the public. People may or may not like it. The page remains unaltered. With this conviction, I began to write about the episode. The late GV Behere, editor of the Painjan, a Marathi monthly magazine, took responsibility for publishing the series. At the end published the series in book form under the title "Gandhiji Hatya Ani Mee" (The Gandhiji and I) in October 1967.

The Government being allergic to the truth that exposed its falsehood, it banned the book two months later. The first edition was almost sold out by then.

Shri Behere and I approached the Supreme Court of Maharashtra, Mumbai, alleging the injustice to our right to freedom of expression. The Court, made up of Modi, VS Desai and Chandrachud JJ, revoked the ban with a unanimous ruling, the 6.8.1969. The sentence was extended to 217 pages.

Then I published other books. The Government kept the declaration of Nathuram Godse. Challenge the injunction by posting the statement, first in Marathi and then in English, and also in other languages. The ban could not survive.

I am associated with the Hindu Mahasabha Akhil Bharat for my political views. As for my family, my daughters were married normally. Also Nana, my son adopted. They all have their respective occupations.

❑

Epilogue

Nathuram Godse's statement covered Gandhiji's policy and actions up to 30.1.1948. If future events corroborated Nathuram's analysis of this as correct or not is a question, and what that policy came to mean to the people of this country is the other. A few words about this, is what I am trying to say as an epilogue.

The 45 years that have elapsed since then only reconfirmed what was declared by Nathuram. The twist of history did not find a single word of this lengthy statement that was erroneous or unjustified.

Gandhiji's physical life ended on 1/30/1948, but the legacy of his politics, serving as he did, the purpose of easily ensuring continuity in power, coupled with with the added benefits of personal aggrandizement and dynastic perpetuation, were conveniently adopted by those at the helm, even if it meant sacrificing the unity of the nation. That the success of the ruler would rest on the welfare of the ruled, was a principle that was now overshadowed by the adoption of the so-called political by Gandhiji.

If India was to be a secular state, where was the need for Pakistan? What if there had to be a vivisection by communal lineage, then where was the need or reason to maintain an anti-Hindu stance under the guise of secularism? Are questions they need an answer.

Secularism, in the true and honest sense of the word, is tolerance towards other belief and nothing else but the Gandhian stigma of secularism, and since it survived as of January 30, 1948, it was not one of tolerance but of appeasement. Despite the inherent failures in this regard and the long-term damage caused by this policy to the nation, such appeasement continues simply because it serves political ends.

Prior to independence, Hindu-Muslim unity was announced as a means and to Swaraj as the end. The medium shattered when the partition was accepted. The Muslims obtained their Swaraj (in Pakistan), and the spectrum presented in India was the secularism.

The leaders, full of ego, did not confess their madness. In a truncated India, Hindu rights had been repressed one after the other by a leadership irresponsible who took refuge behind Gandhian politics. This is what Nathuram Godse had analyzed and predicted, and it is exactly what we are forced to see day after day. day.

Kashmir was called an "ideal Secular State", but Hindus in the valley had already been reduced to almost zero. The attackers now advance towards Jammu to eliminate the Hindu population. This is the result of the fraudulent secularism practiced by leaders at the helm.

Opposition to the settlement in Kashmir of refugees from Pakistan and the subsequent handling of the Kashmir affair has left things in a bad situation. regrettable. All of this is going to be a grotesque and highly volatile legacy and a burden on the generations to come.

Three wars were fought against Pakistan. At what cost and what was the end result? In the last analysis, the problem remains and continues to afflict dangerously.

Saying that a particular Hindu should be discriminated against or denied a right, including respect, because of being born into a particular caste, it was a voice that heard in some neighborhoods, too few in number, but any and wherever these sentiments have been expressed, with the preaching of people like Guru Nanak, Dayanand, Savarkar, and many others, such thoughts began to be effectively neutralized. Nathuram Vinayak Godse was also a firm believer that all men are equal; that caste made no difference and that The only thing that made a difference between man and man was honesty, intelligence and the hard work of the person.

However, ensuring political sinecres and goals was a strategy that required creation of differences by caste lineage. Such schisms were first devised and created, and then the propaganda machine used to blow them out of proportion. A Once such divisions came into being, they were adopted, first a service of "Sympathy", and after that, a policy of "appeasement" for profit politicians. It was with this appearance that such a policy served its best purpose and etiquette Gandhiana created her with mediocre sanctity. But what the followers of Gandhiji seek to achieve is not equality or removal of impediments, but a situation where the caste considerations detract from those of individual competence, hard work and integrity ; as a result of which, the basic criteria pass from skill individual and thus serve the dual purpose of first creating the division, and then completing it with appeasement.

After all, the policy in place meant identifying a section that give hope to serve as a voter bank, start by filling their ears telling them that they have been treated unfairly and sometimes even treating and planting a "Leader" for that section, followed with endless sympathy, and then grant concessions and benefits of public spending and promise them even more, the appeal of more, serving as the ideal hook to ensure the continuity of the vote.

Gandhiji's so-called policy of enhancing the caste and communal division was found it to a convenient extension in the early 1960s when we saw the linguistic vivisection of the country. This was even followed by an attempt at the Sikh-Hindu in the early eighties. Every possible means at his disposal was used to make that criminal and antisocial elements of both communities went down the throat of the other. It is fortunate that people, that is, both Hindus and Sikhs, saw through this game and they would come to realize that all this was nothing but political maneuvering.

The unfortunate trend of *"keeping people poor and uneducated"* is illustrated best for the calculated use of "austerity", as advocated by Gandhiji, to indirectly institutionalize poverty and basic survival of the masses women workers in India, as a means to evade responsibility and public response. Linguistic vivisection only ensured insufficient education for the masses. For keep prosperity growth moderate, the public sector, with its gigantic losses, it was practical.

This enduring poverty, commemorated two and a half decades after the death of Gandhiji, through the slogan of *"Garibi Hatao"* , ensured the easy continuity of those in the power. *"Garibi"* , however, remains stalking the length and breadth of the nation, and to the Garib's consolation , the austere example of Gandhiji is proposed. The public and administrative institutions and companies become worthless. The welfare of the people have lost their meaning. It is what we witness in post-independence India. Laws that were made from time to time provided a number of benefits additional to Muslims, keeping them *"exempt"* from general laws.

These laws, in general terms, were all directed to give excessive advantage to the Muslim community. Apart from the refusal to present a uniform civil code, still in other matters, if the laws formulated from 1950 to date were examined, the *"tint Gandhian"* would be more than evident in the pro-Muslim inclination of such enactments.

For example, laws concerning the Wakf properties of Muslims are had done so to freely cover properties and exempt them from the laws of Roof and Rent, but none of those benefits are given to Hindu institutions. Other Example relates to gifts of property.

The Supreme Court, in the Shah Bano case, adopted a progressive and practice, but the Government wasted no time to alter this criterion, simply because they wanted to keep the minority appeased.

Epilogue

It is strange that they announce the birthday of Prophet Mahammad as well as that of Mahatma Gandhi as national holidays, as no such declaration has been made to *"Ram Naumi"* Lord Ram's birthday.

How illegal immigrants from Pakistan are welcomed and Bangladesh and unauthorized colonies are set up for them, just because they serve as Voter banks is another example of the application of this Gandhian legacy. They go also family planning schemes only against the Hindus.

Even the Indian Archeology Agency doesn't seem to be that kind and benevolent structures of Hindu origin or design as they are with others, and if the statistics, the scope of protection they guarantee will be predominantly Islamic. Structures that in 1700-1947 lay not only abandoned but almost collapsed by the ravages of time, they are restored by vast investments. One wonders what is the source of the funds and how they can be used in the future.

Humanity is not new and it is up to History to write in what has consisted. The last 45 years are still fresh in our memories and the circumstances that prevailed, continue in sharp focus. Truly, The real harmed have been the Hindus of India, the victims have also been the Hindus and, far from correcting a few misplaced practices and rituals that have dragged into the system over the years, today, the goal of those in power continues being divide, subdivide and sub-subdivide. Create conflicts and seek to appease those who serve established political purposes. All this in the fraudulent context of politics supposedly *"Gandhian"*. Being the current objective merely political and even personal.

The *"cult of personality"* in which the factors of reason, logic and assistant of the vote betray, leaving everything to the stubbornness or the ego of the so-called leader, they were a matter of critical to Nathuram, and this is another Gandhian legacy that survives to this day.

Prices have increased multiply, and there has been continuous inflation from 1948 to date. The way the value of the Indian rupee has fallen with respect to to international currencies such as the US dollar or the British pound during this period is a matter that hurts each and every one. Corruption is endemic in daily life, and it is what we see as the end result of the application of such a policy.

The situation of law and order has deteriorated to an alarming extent low, while unemployment is high. Moral degradation is what we see completely. It is irony, of some kind or by fate, that wearing a khadi with a Gandhi cap on top, has come to work by giving the user a license to operate outside the norms of law and morality.

As environmentalists talk about air pollution, how much more has caused in our system this "Gandhian cult" in which the prevailing criminalization of the nation's politics and corruption in the public administration perhaps show some day, some enlightened citizen or some instrument that regulates. The situation unfortunate of the common man and the view that the country presents today, compared to Germany, Japan, Korea or Taiwan have only one Gandhian story to tell.

In the end, all one can say is that Nathuram Godse's statement, Made 45 years ago, it included a warning. That was one of the main reasons for which it was prohibited. If this warning had been heeded, it is possible that the country in general and the Hindus in particular were not in the situation in which found today. Precisely, if India had been achieved as a nation in 45 years post-independence, if this legacy of fraudulent politics and politics had not been forgotten out of place, it would be the economists who elaborated, and not a convict in the case of the assassination of Gandhi whoever did it.

❏

Above: The silver urn in the author's hands contains the ashes of Nathuram Godse and Narayan Apte, who were executed on 15 November 1949, in the Ambala Prison.

Every year on November 15, a meeting is held at the author's residence in Pune to reaffirm the last wish in the will of Nathuram to submerge the ashes in the Sindhu River only when it again freely into Akhand Bharat. Reaffirmation it is also done in many other cities.

The Will

Nathuram's will is in the form of a letter in Hindi, addressed to Shri Dattatraya Vinayak Godse, his younger brother. The Magistrate placed a stamp on November 15, 1949. The prison authorities gave him the letter to Shri Dattatraya.

Nathuram left the only valuable possession, his ashes, and instructed how to dispose of them. The will was in Hindi and a translation into English appears on the next page.

Ambala Jail

My dear Dattatraya,

If you are allowed to perform the last rites on my body, you can do them anyway. But I am going to express along with this a specific wish.

The river Indus (Sindu), on the banks of which our rishis prehistoric people composed the Vedas, it is the border of our Bharatvarsha, that is, Hindustan.

My ashes may sink into the Sacred Sindhu River when it flows again freely under the aegis of the Hindustani flag. That it will be the holy day for us.

It hardly even matters if it takes a couple of generations to realize my wish. Keep my ashes until then, and if that day doesn't come in your lifetime, pass the remains to posterity to translate my wish into reality.

If and when the government lifts the ban in the statement that I did in court, I authorize you to publish it.

11/14/1949   Nathuram Vinayak Godse

I have donated 101 rupees this day for use in the dome (Kalasha) of the sacred Somnath temple under construction.

11/15/1949   Nathuram Vinayak Godse
7.15 am   Magistrate's Seal
                                          Signature and date
                                               11-15-1949

मृत्युपत्र

प्रिय बंधो! चि. दत्तात्रय वि. गोडसे

मेरे बीमा के रुपिया अगर आ जाएँगे तो उस रुपिया का विनिभोग आपके परिवार के कार्य के लिए करना। रु. 2000 आपकी पत्नी के नाम पर। रु. 3000 चि. गोपाल की धर्मपत्नी के नाम पर और रु. 2000 आपके नाम पर। इस तरह से बीमा के कागजों पर मैंने रुपिया मेरी मृत्यु के बाद मिलने के लिए लिखा है।

मेरी उत्तर क्रिया करने का अधिकार अगर आपको मिलेगा तो आप आपकी इच्छा से किसी तरह भी इस शुभ कार्य को समाप्त करना। लेकिन मेरी अंतिम विशेष इच्छा यही लिखता हूँ।

अपने भारत वर्ष की सीमारेखा सिंध नदी है। जिसके किनारों पर वेदों की रचना प्राचीन द्रष्टाओं ने की है। वह सिंधू नदी जिस शुभ दिन में फिर भारत वर्ष के ध्वज की छाया में स्वच्छंदता से बहती रहेगी उन दिनों में मेरी अस्थियों या रक्षा का कुछ छोटा-सा हिस्सा उस सिंधू नदी में बहा दिया जाए।

यह मेरी इच्छा सत्यसृष्टि में आपने के लिए शायद और भी एक दो पीढ़ी (Generations) का समय लग जाए तो भी चिंता नहीं। उस दिन तक वह अवशेष वैसा ही रखो और आपके जीवन में वह शुभ दिन न आए तो आपके वारिसों को ये मेरी अंतिम इच्छा बतलाते जाना।

अगर मेरा न्यायालयीन वक्तव्य कभी सरकार बंध मुक्त करेगी तो उसके प्रकाशन का अधिकार भी मैं आपको दे रहा हूँ।

मैंने 101 रुपिया आपको आज दिए हैं जो आप सौराष्ट्र सोमनाथ मंदिर का पुनरुद्धार हो रहा है उसके कलश कार्य के लिए भेज देना।

(नाथूराम वि. गोडसे)

15.11.93

समय 7.15 प्रात:

आपका शुभेच्छु

नाथूराम वि. गोडसे

14.11.49

Gopal Vinayak Godse
(Sentenced to life in exile.
Released on October 13, 1964)

Naryan Dattatraya Apte
(Both executed on
November 15, 1949, in
The Ambala Prison)

Nathuram Vinayak Godse

Vishnu Ramkrishna Karkare
(Sentenced to life in exile.
Released on October 13, 1964. Died April 6, 1974)

Madan Lal Kashmirilal Pahawa
(Sentenced to life in exile.
Released on October 13, 1964)

Dock of the accused
1. Nathuram Godse, 2. Narayan Apte,3. Vishnu Karkare,
4. Digambar Badge, 5. Madan Lal Pahwa,
6. Gopal Godse, 7. Veer savarkar.
(Sadashiv Parchure and Shankar Kistaya are not seen)

Swatantrya Veer
Vinayak Damodar Savarkar
(Acquitted on February 10, 1949.
Date of birth: May 28, 1883.
Died February 26, 1966)

ISBN: 9789390600274

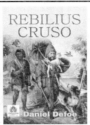

ISBN: 9789390600243

ISBN: 9789390600342

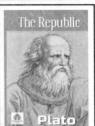

ISBN: 9789390600359

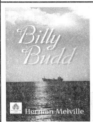

ISBN:9789390600410

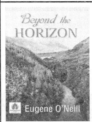

ISBN: 9789390600229

ISBN: 9789390600496

ISBN: 9789390600489

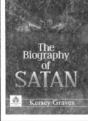

ISBN: 9789390600403

ISBN: 9789390600564

ISBN: 9789390600571

ISBN: 9789390600588

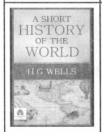

ISBN: 9789390600595

ISBN: 9789390600649

ISBN: 9789390600656

ISBN: 9789390600847

ISBN: 9789390600267

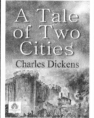

ISBN: 9789390600663

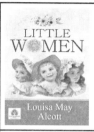

ISBN: 9789390600670

ISBN: 9789390600724

ISBN: 9789390600748

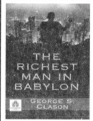

ISBN: 9789390600762

ISBN: 9789390600151

ISBN: 9789390600465

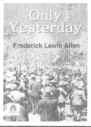

ISBN: 9789390600144

ISBN: 9789390600236

ISBN: 9789390600380

ISBN: 9789390600335

ISBN: 9789390600700

ISBN: 9789390600793

ISBN: 9789390600809

ISBN: 9789390600816

ISBN: 9789390600861

ISBN: 9789390600892

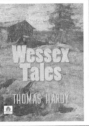

ISBN: 9789390600946

ISBN: 9789390600953

ISBN:9789390600960

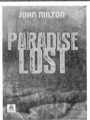

ISBN: 9789390600977

ISBN: 9789390600007

ISBN: 9789390600397

ISBN: 9789390600557

ISBN: 9789390600632

ISBN: 9789390600717

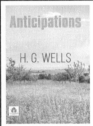

ISBN: 9789390600779

ISBN: 9789390600854

ISBN: 9789390600540

ISBN: 9789390600939

ISBN: 9789390600083